Second Edit

Storytelling
The Secret Sauce
of Fundraising Success

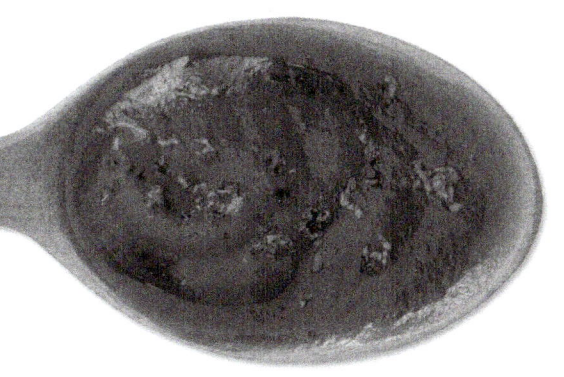

Lynn Malzone Ierardi, JD

https://www.giftplanningadvisor.com

What Others Are Saying...

People want to help, and want to give. A good story can move them from wanting to doing, and Lynn Malzone Ierardi's wonderful book blends the latest science with her extensive experience to show readers how stories facilitate fundraising.
   Paul J. Zak
   Professor, Claremont Graduate University and CEO, Immersion Neuroscience

Lynn's book will satisfy your hunger for the importance of storytelling and provide a recipe for success. Throughout each chapter you will discover ingredients that enable you to whip up the special sauce that is your charity's mission. Then you can go out and share it with the world. Bon appetit!
   Alexandra Pia Brovey
   Author of *Zen and the Art of Fundraising: 8 Pillars of Success*, *Zen and the Art of Fundraising: 8 MORE Pillars of Success*, and *Zen and the Art of Fundraising: The Pillars In Practice*

Lynn's book is an excellent guide to navigating the unique world of philanthropic storytelling. Through a number of vivid examples and amusing anecdotes, she shares powerful advice for anyone interested in becoming a better fundraiser. I've already begun to integrate a number of her recommendations into my own work as a digital communicator.
   Johanna Humphrey
   Director of Digital Communications
   University of Pennsylvania Development and Alumni Relations

Storytelling is such a powerful way we can connect with our donors. Sharing stories is one of the most effective fundraising tools we have at The Nature Conservancy to create passion for our mission and saving the planet. Lynn's book is filled with practical tips, techniques, and best practices for embedding storytelling into the fabric of our organizations.
   Jackie W. Franey
   Director of Gift Planning Fundraising
   The Nature Conservancy

I was lucky to be Lynn's frequent partner in fundraising during my time at the University of Pennsylvania and what she has accomplished with this book is sharing with you not only the true secret sauce of how to be a successful fundraiser, but also how to find the humor and joy while executing the 'art of the ask.' Oh, and it's sauce, not gravy, per my Italian grandmother!

    Pamela Peters Arms
    Real Estate Banking Vice President

Storytelling: The Secret Sauce of Fundraising Success *is an amazing read! Every fundraiser should spend time reading and digesting its insightful content. It will help them achieve greater success.*

    Eddie Thompson
    CEO and Founder
    Thompson & Associates

The point of instructional writing is to provide high utility, but that doesn't mean it has to be dry and boring. Lynn Malzone Ierardi has demonstrated that quite skillfully in her book on how to better use stories to succeed at charitable fundraising and, big surprise, she does it by providing about a dozen compelling stories. This is a must-read for anyone engaged in the field, but it's also a pleasurable read.

    Jason Huffman
    Heavily seasoned (pun intended) food journalist
    and currently senior fish reporter for Undercurrent News

This book turns theory into reality. It converts complexity into practical tactics. Making this a reality requires a special person. It requires an in-the-trenches fundraising superstar. It requires someone who actually knows what it takes to capture multi-million-dollar gifts. It requires someone who understands the deep transactional complexity of complex mega gifts. And, more importantly, it requires someone who understands how to keep that complexity from killing the giving motivation. It requires someone like Lynn.

    Russell James III, JD, PhD., CFP®
    Professor
    Director of Graduate Studies in Charitable Financial Planning
    The CH Foundation Chair in Personal Financial Planning
    Texas Tech University
    Lubbock, Texas

Storytelling: The Secret Sauce of Fundraising Success
Second Edition

Lynn Malzone Ierardi, JD

All rights reserved. No part of this book shall be reproduced, stored in a retrieval system, or transmitted by any means, electronic, mechanical, photocopying, recording, or otherwise, without written permission from the publisher. No patent liability is assumed with respect to the use of the information contained herein. This publication contains the opinions and ideas of its author. It is intended to provide helpful and informative material on the subject matter covered. It is sold with the understanding that the author and publisher are not engaged in rendering professional services in the book. If the reader requires personal assistance or advice, a competent professional should be consulted. The author and publisher specifically disclaim any responsibility for any liability, loss, or risk, personal or otherwise, that is incurred as a consequence, directly or indirectly, of the use and application of any of the contents of this book. Although every precaution has been taken in the preparation of this book, the publisher and author assume no responsibility for errors or omissions. No liability is assumed for damages resulting from the use of information contained herein.

Published by Gift Planning Advisor

Copyright © 2021 Lynn Malzone Ierardi, JD

ISBN Print Book: 978-1-7366900-0-0

Library of Congress Control Number: 2021944328

13 12 11 10 9 8 7 6 5 4 3 2 1

About the Author

Lynn Malzone Ierardi, JD has been in the gift and estate planning field for more than thirty years. She is a leader in the charitable planning community. Lynn was elected Chair of the Board of the National Association of Charitable Gift Planners (CGP) after serving terms as Treasurer and Chair-elect. She has been a member of CGP since 1993 and is a member of the CGP Leadership Institute.

She is a past board member, conference chair, and past President of the New Jersey Council of Charitable Gift Planners, a current board member of the Planned Giving Council of Greater Philadelphia, and a regular faculty member for the Planned Giving Course.

As the Director of Gift Planning for the University of Pennsylvania (Penn), Lynn worked with several schools and centers and handled gifts of real estate university-wide. She has served as an independent consultant to a variety of nonprofit organizations through her firm, Gift Planning Advisor, founded in 2002.

Prior to joining Penn, she held gift planning positions in health and higher education, served as Vice President with the Merrill Lynch Center for Philanthropy, and practiced estate planning, tax, and real estate law.

After graduating from Lycoming College with a BA in English, Spanish, and Literature, she received her Juris Doctor from Fordham University School of Law. A dynamic and highly rated speaker, Lynn has presented at conferences, meetings, and webinars throughout the United States and in the United Kingdom on a variety of gift planning topics. She has also been a contributor to several gift planning publications, including *Planned Giving Today*.

She is the *Proud Penn Parent* of two adult daughters, Katie and Kristen, and lives with her favorite storyteller and husband, Mark, in Philadelphia. When not wearing a gift planning hat, Lynn enjoys wearing sunglasses on the beach, dancing the night away, or watching some of the most magnificent sunsets in the world at Lake Naomi. She has served as a member of the Lake Naomi Finance Committee and the Lake Naomi Board of Governors.

Dedication

I dedicate this book to my husband, Mark, and my daughters, Katie and Kristen. I love you more than you will ever know, and appreciate everything you do to stir the pot, simmer the sauce, and create the story that is my life. I also dedicate this book to my brother, Tony, who, at six foot three with a big personality to match, was one of the biggest inspirations for me to write this book.

Author's Acknowledgments

I want to acknowledge my friends on the National Association of Charitable Gift Planners board (current and past) and my colleagues at the University of Pennsylvania, particularly the gift planning team. You have all helped me to grow both professionally and personally.

I give special thanks to my original publisher, Stephen Nill, for his patience (especially when I asked for more time) and support. I warmly thank Alexandra Pia Brovey for nudging me along to write this book. I would never have taken on this project but for her loyal friendship and encouragement.

I thank the following colleagues and friends for reviewing my manuscript: Pamela Peters Arms, Alexandra Pia Brovey, Jackie W. Franey, Jason Huffman, Johanna Humphrey, Kristen Ierardi, Russell James, Cathy Reagan Sheffield, and Eddie Thompson. Thanks to Jane Puttanniah for the great cover design.

I thank Adam M. Grant for the time and suggestions he gave me as a "newbie" author. Adam lives by the advice he offers in his books and blogs and is a giver in every sense of the word.

I thank the people and organizations featured in this book for generously sharing your storytelling expertise and experiences with me. I couldn't have completed the project without your insights.

I thank my mom for always being my biggest fan. She encouraged me to think I could do anything if I put my mind to it. When I was growing up, we would always "figure out a way" even when there didn't seem to be a path forward. She was busy studying for exams after she worked all day and put my brother and me to bed. My mom had *grit* long before anyone wrote articles or books about it. She gave me that gift.

I thank my father and stepmom, Anthony and Kathy, for sharing their love and their thirst for learning with me. They taught me to appreciate art, books, music—and so much more. Dad taught me how to hit a quarter swinging on a string with a BB gun and how to throw a great football pass. I was always picked to play quarterback in co-ed gym class, and my love of football allowed me to win the Lake Naomi football pool—twice.

My parents—all three of them—raised me to think about graduate school, not just college, at a time when some girls weren't lucky enough to have that kind of support. Thank you for instilling that confidence in me and setting the bar high.

I lovingly acknowledge my husband, Mark J. Ierardi, JD, CPA. He's been my best friend and my favorite storyteller since our law school days. Over the last thirty years, we have built a rock-solid marriage, created a beautiful family, raised two amazing daughters, successfully navigated our careers, and enjoyed the company of great friends. Our story has included so many joys, some challenges, and a few deep sorrows. I would do it all over again because he is truly *my happily ever after.*

I thank my beautiful daughters, Katie and Kristen, who are the center of my universe. They keep me on my toes by being such smart, strong, and independent women. They each made me a *Proud Penn Parent,* and I'm awestruck by their achievements. I have every confidence they will make the world a better place. I look forward with great excitement to the next chapters of *your* stories.

Finally, I thank my brother, Tony. Missing him is a constant reminder to focus on what's important, and that there is no such thing as plenty of time. Life is way too short—eat dessert first.

Contents

Foreword xvii

Introduction 1

Chapter One 5
The Menu: Introduction to Delicious Stories

Chapter Two 13
The Recipe for the Secret Sauce: Key Ingredients for a Good Story

Chapter Three 23
Shopping for the Perfect Ingredients: Finding Your Stories

Chapter Four 29
Serving up the Entrée: Sharing Your Stories

Chapter Five 35
Variations on the Recipe: Adding Spice to Your Stories

Chapter Six 43
The Side Dishes: The Many Ways Stories Can Be Served

Chapter Seven 51
The Kitchen Mishap: Navigating Change with Storytelling

Chapter Eight 59
Hell's Kitchen: The Inferno that Triggered a Seismic Change

Chapter Nine 69
The Dessert: Sweet Success Stories

Chapter Ten 77
Check Please! Summary and Additional Resources

Appendix A 81
Story Collection Form

Appendix B 83
Sample Consent Form

Appendix C 85
Storytelling Culture Assessment Form

Appendix D 89
Resources

Summary of Chapters

Introduction 1

Chapter One 5

The Menu: Introduction to Delicious Stories. Storytelling has been around since the beginning of time, and it has been the subject of significant research and discussion. Stories bind us together and capture our history. Storytelling is essential to our lives and, if used effectively, it has the potential to make us better fundraisers and communicators.

Chapter Two 13

The Recipe for the Secret Sauce: Key Ingredients for a Good Story. Some ingredients are essential. You just can't make a good sauce (or gravy as my grandfather called it) without tomatoes. What ingredients engage the audience and have an impact? What flavors will spark the appetite and make your mouth water?

Chapter Three 23

Shopping for the Perfect Ingredients: Finding Your Stories. Now that you have your list of ingredients, where should you shop? Most people look to a variety of sources for the freshest ingredients, and you should do the same when gathering stories. Start with your donors, but don't stop there. Patience and passion can assist us in navigating multi-year and multi-asset gifts.

Chapter Four 29

Serving up the Entrée: Sharing Your Stories. Great stories will help you to raise more money and engage donors. The most important story for a nonprofit to share is the story of your mission—the *why* you exist. A good mission story will answer questions such as: What problem are you solving? What impact will you have? How can your donors and friends be a part of the solution? What effect does your work have on people's lives? This is your entrée!

Chapter Five 35

Variations on the Recipe: Adding Spice to Your Stories. Historically, all storytelling was oral. Speaking is still perhaps the best format for storytelling—especially for fundraisers. Avoid text-heavy PowerPoint slides or fact-heavy conversation that can make speech bland. Good stories add the spice and flavor that make you a better speaker and therefore a better fundraiser.

Chapter Six 43

The Side Dishes: The Many Ways Stories Can Be Served. The *method* of delivery is an integral part of the recipe. My meatballs are always baked. Some people insist the only way to make meatballs is to fry them. Stories have been adapted to many formats—music, film, and social media are just a few examples. The recipe of a story must be adjusted by the storyteller to target the audience.

Chapter Seven 51

The Kitchen Mishap: Navigating Change with Storytelling. There will always be obstacles and changes—it's inevitable! There will be tax law changes, fluctuations in the economy (e.g., a Great Recession), or redirection of the strategic plan. One surefire way to successfully navigate obstacles and changes is to share your stories. For every change in the recipe, storytelling is the constant.

Chapter Eight 59

Hell's Kitchen: The Inferno that Triggered a Seismic Change. This was no kitchen mishap. The place nearly burned to the ground! In 2020, a global pandemic, civil unrest, and political turmoil provoked change at a pace and on a level that was previously unimaginable.

In response, nonprofit organizations stepped up to increased demands, pivoted, and persevered—thereby producing amazing stories of tenacity, creativity, and triumph. To survive and thrive, the most successful nonprofit organizations will continue to hone their storytelling skills and position themselves for the next wave of inevitable change.

Chapter Nine 69

The Dessert: Sweet Success Stories. Stories of success are the sweetest. A thank-you story can be like a rich dessert that's easy to share and worth saving room for. Sharing the impact of gifts through stories is a great way to cultivate and steward donors.

Chapter Ten 77

Check Please! Summary and Additional Resources. Not every meal will provide the dining experience you hope for—and not every story will result in a gift. Each one is, however, an opportunity to learn and improve. So, the story can continue. It doesn't end here.

Foreword

This book is a joy for me. Sharing some of *my* stories helps explain why. As a professor, my research is focused on one goal: how can we encourage generosity? Pursuing that one goal has led me to many investigative methods. Econometric analysis of large national datasets? Yes. Laboratory experiments? Yes. Field experiments? Yes. Online experiments? Yes. Neuroimaging? Yes. Skin conductance response? Yes. In-depth qualitative interviews? Yes. But answering research questions is not just about data. It's also about theory. Theory from economics, sociology, psychology, neuroscience, law, communication, anthropology, human development, and linguistics.

And at the end of that long, complicated process, what is the result? What's the answer? The answer is *story*. The answer is connecting the charity's story with the donor's life story.

Consider this example. The largest single charitable contribution for many people will be a gift in their will. We had a group of people make these charitable decisions in an experiment. But to make it interesting, they did this while in an fMRI brain scanner. What did we see? When people make these decisions, their neural activations can be described as "visualized autobiography." The greater the visualization, the greater the interest in making a gift.

In qualitative interviews, when people were asked why they selected particular charities to be in their wills, what did they talk about? They talked about connections with their life story.

When we tested a range of messages to encourage such gifts, what worked best? Stories. Brief stories of how others like the reader had included gifts that reflected their own life stories.

And when we looked for the best phrasing to add to a request for such gifts, what worked? Life stories. Not just asking about a gift in a will. But rather, asking about a gift in a will "to support causes that have been important in your life."

Powerful fundraising connects the charity's story with the donor's life story. I like to say that you need to know only one rule: advance the donor's hero story. The answer is *story*.

But there is a problem with academic research. As academics, we love to focus on the "Why?" questions. We love the hypertechnical explanations. (And I'm guilty. I'll happily spend all afternoon telling you why the first derivative of my mathematical economic model explains charitable motivations for gifts in wills.) But, fundraisers don't need answers to just the "Why?" questions. Fundraisers need answers to the "How?" questions. How can I do this? How can I change my work? How can I get better right now?

This is where Lynn Malzone Ierardi delivers the goods. This book turns theory into reality. It converts complexity into practical tactics. Making this a reality requires a special person. It requires an in-the-trenches fundraising superstar. It requires someone who actually knows what it takes to capture multi-million-dollar gifts. It requires someone who understands the deep transactional complexity of complex mega gifts. And, more importantly, it requires someone who understands how to keep that complexity from killing the giving motivation. It requires someone like Lynn.

We live in a business world that focuses on the value proposition. Let me offer you an unbeatable value proposition. Suppose you want to capture more than thirty years' worth of expertise in the real world of complex and major gifts. Suppose you want that knowledge from a career at the largest and most respected institutions on the planet. You have two options. You can spend thirty years learning by trial and error. Or you can spend the afternoon with this book. I recommend the latter.

Inspiring generosity in others is a noble calling. If you are reading this, you are likely part of that noble calling. Your service can advance the important causes where you work. But, it does more. Your work can transform the donors' lives as well. Thank you for making the choice to pursue this noble calling. Thank you for caring enough to get better at doing it by learning from one of the best. Thank you for wisely investing your time by reading this book.

Russell James III, JD, PhD., CFP®
Professor
Director of Graduate Studies in Charitable Financial Planning
The CH Foundation Chair in Personal Financial Planning
Texas Tech University
Lubbock, Texas

Introduction

Storytelling is a great tool for nonprofit organizations. We have amazing stories to share—stories of perseverance, fortitude, and generosity. These stories give us a voice to compete in a world that gets noisier every day, where people are looking for ways to find meaning and connection. Scientific research confirms good storytelling is one of the most powerful ways to engage stakeholders and influence behavior.

After all, who doesn't love a good story? If we're lucky, as small children our love for stories begins as we savor the tales our parents read aloud. Perhaps we heard stories from our grandparents, too. Soon, we learn to read, and we experience the joy of devouring stories. I can vividly recall some of the books I read as a child and my favorite authors as a teen. Judy Blume, author of *Are You There God? It's Me, Margaret,* was my idol for a few years.

The years passed, and I became the storyteller for my own children, Katie and Kristen. I can only imagine how many times I read aloud *The Foot Book* by Dr. Seuss or *Goodnight Moon* by Margaret Wise Brown. Then, in what now seems like an instant, they were reading on their own and relishing stories and inviting me to step into their experiences.

When Katie was about seven years old, she devoured every book in the series about Sheltie the Shetland Pony by Peter Clover. *Sheltie Goes to School, Sheltie to the Rescue, Sheltie in Double Trouble*...she read them all. One night, I walked into her bedroom to say goodnight, and she was weeping in her bed.

"Oh, my goodness, what's the matter, Katie?" I asked. Sobbing, she said, "Sheltie fell through the ice when he tried to save Emma, and he might die!"

Just as the stories of Sheltie had transported Katie to a wonderful world of ponies and adventures, this story now took her to a place of pain and sadness. Sheltie didn't die, but it was touch-and-go for a while. It's incredible how a story has the power to captivate us and transport us to a place where we become one with the story.

This power is biological. Humans have shared stories since we started speaking and then discovered the ability to paint on cave walls and etch stone tablets.

Can you remember a time when a story transported you? Perhaps it was something classic like Shakespeare or Edgar Allen Poe (*The Cask of Amontillado* is one of my favorites). Maybe it was something more current like a Nicholas Sparks or John Grisham book. Or maybe it wasn't a book at all but a Steven Spielberg or Francis Ford Coppola movie.

Storytelling is fundamental to our daily lives. Stories serve as the common thread of families and traditions. All day long we share stories with each other. Stories about who took a hit on the soccer field after school, how rough the commute was because the train was stuck in a tunnel for forty minutes, or gossip in the office about an affair going on upstairs. We bond over stories that include rich details and intense emotions. Think about the story of a loved one who faced a challenge that had a lasting impact on your family. How many of us have been impacted, for example, by cancer?

The incredible power of stories became painfully apparent to me in 2017 when my brother, Tony, was diagnosed with esophageal cancer.

We raced to Penn Medicine in Philadelphia, where I knew he would get the best possible care. But the cancer was far too advanced, and it was too late to help him. In just three weeks, he was gone. I was devastated and heartbroken. As I prepared the eulogy and video for his memorial, I knew that his story would be one of the most important and difficult ones I'd ever share.

The stories that people share about you are the legacy that you leave behind when you're gone. Stories, unlike people, can live forever.

It was profoundly important for me to tell Tony's story, as it would be a part of his lasting legacy. I shared stories about his strength, his sense of humor, his integrity, and his generosity. From the time Tony was a small child, he loved to drive. He drove toy cars, go-carts, and bicycles, then cars, trucks, and motorcycles. He loved anything on wheels. In the last decade of his life, he closed his business and fulfilled his dream of driving tractor-trailers.

A few months before Tony died, he was stopped at a red light. He checked his mirrors one last time before making the turn and suddenly noticed a man's feet sticking out from under the truck. A homeless man had rolled off the center median, and he was seconds away from being crushed under the wheels of Tony's tractor-trailer. Tony got out of his truck, helped him up, and told him he needed to find a safer spot to sleep than the center median. He was rattled by the incident. So, he went back a few days later to look for the man. He found him in the very same spot. Tony again suggested that he find a safe spot, and this time gave him food, water, and Girl Scout Cookies.

Tony had more than enough Girl Scout Cookies to share after purchasing one-hundred boxes from our little cousin. He had given out boxes at work, mailed them to soldiers, and now given them to a homeless man. When Tony shared the story with me, he said, "Lynn, some people are just stuck. I may not have a lot, but when I look at my life and my family, I know I have a lot."

I still can't believe he's gone.

The stories of our childhood, our close bond, our family, and our life experiences will be with me forever. They are stored in my memory bank and are far more valuable to me than any material possession. This difficult experience inspired me to learn more about storytelling—and to write this book.

As I began writing, I quickly realized it is a hot topic. It's all over the internet, in books, magazines, and newspapers. There are online storytelling courses and even storytelling conferences. But storytelling isn't a fad. It has been around for a long time, and it's not going away. If anything, the role of storytelling is more important than ever. Businesses are keenly aware of the fact that people have short attention spans, and they must do something to grab our attention and our wallets. They realize that storytelling has a significant effect on their bottom line.

The nonprofit world is no different. Stories are at the core of *why* nonprofit organizations exist. Storytelling is *especially* crucial for effective fundraising. You're likely already familiar with the fundraising cycle (cultivate, ask, steward, and repeat). As you follow those steps, you are raising awareness and building relationships. The storytelling cycle achieves these same goals by following a similar cycle: plan, collect, develop, share, evaluate, and repeat.

Storytelling should come naturally to nonprofit fundraisers and communicators. Too often, it doesn't happen that way.

Like a good meal, storytelling can be delicious if it is executed with a bit of strategy. It requires planning the meal, choosing and collecting the right ingredients, and then sharing the meal with the right people, in the right setting, and at the right time. According to Lisa Cron, the author of *Wired for Story*, "stories feel good for the same reason food tastes good—because without it we couldn't survive."

I hope this book will provide you with food for thought and help you to be a more effective storyteller.

Chapter One

The Menu: Introduction to Delicious Stories

It has been said that next to hunger and thirst, our most basic human need is for storytelling.

—**Khalil Gibran**

The hospital system in Southern California was in trouble. It was looking for ways to cut expenses, and there was a very real possibility one of the only trauma centers in the region would close. The gap in emergency coverage for the region would translate to a devastating impact on California citizens and precious lives lost.

The development team needed to raise significant revenue to keep the trauma center open. But how could they craft a message about the trauma center that would be compelling for prospective donors, particularly for those without an existing relationship with the hospital?

By sharing a story. Not just any story, but a *video* of a helicopter landing on the hospital's helipad bringing in a little boy who was impaled by a chainsaw. He was bleeding profusely, and his airway was compromised. He was barely alive by the time the helicopter landed. The hospital already had the video, but it had never been used to engage donors and prospects. Stephen Nill, the Senior Vice President of Development, and his team were about to change that.

Whenever possible, the development team shared the video with donors and prospects (with permission, of course) complete with surround sound and booming speakers that captured the *whap-whap* of the helicopter coming in for a landing. It was so realistic that some members of the audience would duck before realizing the sound was coming from the video.

The story had a happy ending—a picture of the boy smiling for the camera. But the key ingredient to this story was that the trauma surgeons were able to save the boy's life only because the trauma center was so close.

Had there been no local trauma center, the outcome would have been radically different.

It was a compelling story because it included the essential ingredients of a good story, it offered donors a reason to care, and perhaps most importantly, it provided donors an opportunity to be the heroes. Perhaps they could see themselves, their children, or their grandchildren in that video. The story proved to be *the secret sauce of fundraising success*. Community members stepped forward with significant gifts (many millions in the space of two years) and saved the trauma center. Countless lives were saved. All because of the power of a *story*.

Storytelling makes us human—and that's part of what makes it so delicious! Since the beginning of time, from cave paintings and hieroglyphics to great novels, plays, and movies, we have consumed stories like daily bread to connect with each other and with the world around us. Stories raise awareness, change behavior, and trigger generosity.

One of the first people in America to use storytelling for the public good was Benjamin Franklin. He established an array of organizations and structures that benefitted society, including the first zoo, the first public library, the first fire department, the first public hospital, and (Hurrah! Hurrah! Penn Quakers!) The University of Pennsylvania. Franklin leveraged the technology of his day—printing—to share stories and raise funds for what he deemed to be worthy causes. He has sometimes been referred to as America's first blogger and social networker.

More recently, stories have taken different forms that include TED talks and YouTube videos, blogs, and so much more. Whatever the format, storytelling makes us human and sets us apart from other species.

Stories have been written, printed, blogged, shared, discussed, debated, and passed down through the generations. Why? Because people have an incredible appetite for stories.

We love to take a big bite of a story and savor the tasty details. Stories, in so many ways, satisfy a hunger that we can't deny. Our brains create and crave stories all day long. Even as we sleep, our minds are creating stories in the form of dreams. They permeate every aspect of how we live and how we think. What makes stories so delicious is the way we respond to them. A story triggers an intellectual response. We understand the facts and circumstances presented in a story. It's logical.

But a *good* story does a whole lot more. It also triggers a physical response.

Functional MRI studies have shown that when you're lost in a good story, the same parts of your brain light up that would light up if *you* were actually part of the story. A good story arouses our curiosity. It penetrates the walls of our natural defense systems. It infiltrates our subconscious and becomes memorable.

Maya Angelou said, "I've learned that people will forget what you said, people will forget what you did, but people will never forget how you made them feel." Good stories trigger *feelings*—such as happiness, sadness, anger, or empathy. Perhaps most importantly, a good story influences our behavior. We understand, remember, and share them.

Stories Catalog History, Culture, and Values

The Bible, the Koran, and the Torah include some of the earliest and best examples of storytelling. Captured on the pages are stories of people, places, and events that were shared and passed down orally from generation to generation long before they were written on paper.

Before humans could write, we had to rely on good storytellers (often clergy, politicians, and other leaders) to capture our history. Myths, fables, and folktales all played a role in preserving human history. They were also an effective tool to preserve and pass along culture and values.

People return to the same stories over and over again to find out what happens next. Did they rescue the children? Did they slay the dragon? What happened in that great battle? What's the lesson to be learned?

Stories Ensure Our Survival

We learn from stories as we hear about how the characters solved a problem, how they challenged and defeated an opponent, or how they survived a difficult situation. By sharing what we have learned with others, we can teach valuable and lasting lessons.

Tales dating back to the 6th century BC are attributed to an ancient Greek storyteller known as Aesop. Before *Aesop's Fables* were written, they were passed through many generations orally, and survive to this day.

One of the best-known tales is *The Tortoise and the Hare*. In case you haven't heard it in a while, I'll give you a quick refresher: The hare boasts about how fast he is and challenges the other animals to a race. The tortoise says "sure, bring it!" and they line up at the starting line. The hare bolts out far ahead of the tortoise and thinks he's got it all wrapped up. So, he decides to stop and take a nap. When he wakes up, he's unable to beat the tortoise to the finish line because slow and steady wins the race! Certainly, a valuable lesson.

Stories can also help us to avoid making critical—even life-threatening—mistakes. When Princess Diana died tragically in a car crash in Paris in 1997, my daughters, Katie and Kristen, were both young and impressionable. The story of the accident was all over the news—you couldn't avoid it—and we talked about what happened. One particular detail resonated with my daughters: Princess Diana was not wearing a seat belt when the car crashed violently into the wall of the Paris tunnel. Would she have survived if she had been wearing a seat belt?

A computer simulation of the accident performed by an engineering firm for CNN soon after the crash indicated that seat belts may very well have "turned the fatal crash into one that was very survivable." As the driver recklessly sped up to avoid the paparazzi in hot pursuit, Diana's bodyguard fastened his seat belt. He was the only survivor of the crash.

Deborah Norville, a broadcast journalist, said at the time, "It may be one of the great legacies that she has left the world, something as simple as *buckle your seat belt*." The story of Diana's death resonated because it was so tragic.

> *Storytelling is a very old human skill that gives us an evolutionary advantage. If you can tell young people how you kill an emu, acted out in song or dance, or that Uncle George was eaten by a croc over there, don't go there to swim, then those young people don't have to find out by trial and error.*
>
> **—Margaret Atwood**

It certainly had a lasting impact in our home! For many years after hearing that story, Katie and Kristen would buckle up quickly whenever we got into the car. I never had to remind them to wear their seat belts again. It is an elementary example of how stories can increase our chances of survival.

In the mid-1800's, the City of London lacked a proper sewage system, and the resulting stench was horrible. Cholera was an epidemic, and people believed the disease was spread by breathing bad air. John Snow, said to be one of the first epidemiologists, knew cholera wasn't spread by this "miasma" or bad air, but he couldn't convince the public officials, other doctors, or the people living in the city despite the convincing data he collected. He studied hospital records and tracked the cholera infection.

During a particularly severe outbreak, Snow even documented the fact that a group of brewery workers had avoided getting sick by drinking beer instead of the local water (remember this story in case you need an excuse to drink beer instead of water). He carefully created a map that tracked the infection to the water supply—at the Broad Street pump. He engaged the local preacher to share the story and help convince people that the real problem was in the water. With the map and the story of the brewery workers, he finally convinced the public officials to take the handle off the pump. His story saved many lives.

Stories Are *Powerful*

Study after study supports the conclusion that stories are far more persuasive than facts or data. We are more guarded when we hear facts or data because our brains are wired to be defensive and skeptical of that kind of information. It's much easier to tune out or turn away.

When you hear a good story, however, you are more open and receptive. Stories penetrate your natural defense system and become more compelling and memorable. This is not just because we are entertained by stories. It's great to use stories to escape—a good movie sure makes a rainy afternoon more enjoyable.

But the power of story goes far beyond entertainment.

Businesses are keenly aware of the power of story. Consumers don't just buy products, they buy brands, and they buy stories. Business strategy is all about stories. Coke and Nike know that it's not about soda or sneakers, but about the feelings they can create about their products with their stories.

According to Murray Nossel, cofounder of Narrativ, which teaches storytelling techniques to executives at companies like Disney, Time Warner, and Radisson Hotels, and author of *Powered by Storytelling: Excavate, Craft, and Present Stories to Transform Business Communication*, companies are increasingly recognizing how storytelling affects their bottom line. Nossel believes stories allow customers to "get" the value of a product on an emotional and sensory level.

There is scientific evidence to explain why this is true. Researchers have looked at the impact of stories on the brain and have discovered that it is wired for stories. We can't resist!

A Good Story Is Like a Hug—or a Delicious Meal

Dr. Paul Zak is the Director of the Center for Neuroeconomic Studies at Claremont Graduate University and cofounder and CEO of Immersion Neuroscience. He was one of the first to study the role of oxytocin in human experiences and behaviors. Things like sharing a meal together, hugs, kisses (and yes, sex!) increase the oxytocin levels in both our brains and in our blood; hence Zak and others refer to oxytocin as "the love hormone." Zak also studied how our brains respond to stories.

In one of his studies, the researchers shared the story with the study participants of a father and his two-year-old son, Ben, who has terminal brain cancer. The story has a classic dramatic arc in which the father is struggling to enjoy his son, who is happily playing in the background, while knowing that the child has only a few months to live.

The story concludes with the father resolving to find the strength to be happy "until he takes his last breath." In the study, the story caused an increase in oxytocin in the participants, which had a direct correlation with feelings of empathy for Ben and his father.

They were able to build a predictive model of donations to a childhood cancer charity—the measure of story impact. The model predicted whether a participant would donate money with 82 percent accuracy—and the vast majority of the participants did just that after hearing Ben's story.

I spoke with Dr. Zak about his more recent work with his own company, Immersion Neuroscience. After nearly two decades of research, they are accurately predicting the effectiveness of live events, corporate training modules, movies, and even commercials.

Using a wrist-based neurosensor like an Apple Watch or an eye tracking device, they measure physical responses to stories. By studying what kinds of stories are effective, they can predict the likelihood of someone taking action (including buying a product or making a gift to charity) after hearing a story.

For several years, Zak has used the Immersion Neuroscience platform to study people watching Super Bowl commercials to test and prove the value of the message. At the cost of $5 million for a thirty-second advertisement, this is huge. In a nutshell, the research indicates the commercials that elicit the best response include a story.

That story must include two things: the commercial must grab your attention, and it must elicit emotion that makes you care.

It turns out that stories, even in their simplest forms, can trigger our brains to release oxytocin much like a hug or a delicious meal. For fundraisers, perhaps the most important takeaway is that increasing oxytocin levels make people more likely to donate money to charity. It may not be appropriate to hug all our donors and prospects, but we can certainly tell them a good story (and maybe take them to lunch!).

The best stories are engaging and compelling; we don't just hear those stories, we *feel* them. We know in our gut when we hear a great story—and we are easily distracted and disenchanted when a story doesn't include key ingredients. What are the key ingredients? In the chapters that follow, you'll read about recipes and ingredients to make *your* stories the secret sauce of your own fundraising success.

Chapter Two

The Recipe for the Secret Sauce: Key Ingredients for a Good Story

Tell me the facts and I'll learn. Tell me the truth and I'll believe. But tell me a story and it will live in my heart forever.

—**Native American Proverb**

Spoiler alert: storytelling is not an exact science. There is not one single recipe that guarantees a great meal that everyone will enjoy. People like a variety of flavors based on personal taste. But every story has a basic structure.

In 1863, German dramatist Gustav Freytag described the structure (ingredients) of a good story as the exposition (with rising action), climax, and denouement (after falling action). To put it more simply, according to Aristotle, every story has a beginning, a middle, and an end.

That sounds easy, right? Yet somehow, there are too many stories that are bland and tasteless because they don't include the right ingredients. When you take a bite of story, it should make you say, "mmm…that's good!"

The human mind yields helplessly to the seduction of story according to Jonathan Gottschall, author of *The Storytelling Animal: How Stories Make Us Human.* No matter how hard we concentrate, no matter how deep we dig in our heels, we just can't resist the gravity of alternate worlds. That's why we can't put the book down or turn off Netflix when it's well past midnight, and we know we should be sleeping. Our appetite for the experience is too difficult to curb.

He describes the experience that inspired him to write his book. Driving down the road listening to a song called "Stealing Cinderella," about a little girl who has now grown up and left her father behind, he suddenly must pull over to the side of the road to wipe away his tears. The song triggered deep emotions for him because it made him *feel* the emotion of the storyteller as he thought about the day when his own daughters would leave him behind.

This is what psychologists refer to as narrative transportation. When you identify with a character in a story, and when you feel what you believe they are feeling, you are transported by a compelling story.

We've all been there. Even when we know a story is a fiction—the blood and danger isn't real, or the dog isn't really dying—we still react with a scream or tears. When you enter into a story, you enter into an altered mental state—a state of high suggestibility. Your brain doesn't respond like a spectator, but like a participant. If the character is fearful, you *feel* fearful. We know the danger isn't real, we know it's crazy to believe, but our brains process it as if it's real.

When we are engrossed in a good story, our minds quiet and our attention is focused. When we get lost in a great story, it has the most impact.

There are many opinions, articles, and books about what ingredients make a story compelling. But in the simplest of recipes, you start the story by introducing the characters and describing their situation. The story builds with conflict, tension, and emotion, to a climactic moment, and ultimately, resolution.

Light up Your Taste Buds!

There are variations on the recipe, of course, but it's universally accepted that a compelling story must have a hook. The story should start with something that grabs attention. Consider starting your story with a startling fact or statistic, a prop, or something entertaining or unusual that captures the attention of the audience and draws them in. An intriguing headline might be enough to do it. Or you might start with a "what-if" proposition as Steve Jobs did when he said, "What if you could put a thousand songs in your pocket?" That was surely an attention grabber at the time!

What if the immune system could be reprogrammed to fight cancer? Guess what? It's possible, and it's happening here at Penn. This attention-grabbing headline was used to preview a story about the great work of Dr. Carl June (described in more detail in **Chapter Six**). A startling statistic might give your audience pause: *By 2050, the oceans will contain more plastic than fish.* Combined with an image, a good headline can be a great way to pull the audience in.

Members of the *Plastic Pollution Coalition* have used these very effective hooks to draw in audiences to share stories about the devastating impact of ocean pollution. *Plastic bag vs. jellyfish—if it's difficult for you to tell the difference, imagine how hard it is for a hungry sea turtle!*

ID 123981267 © Przemyslaw Ceglarek | Dreamstime.com

Human beings have short attention spans. Some research suggests that we start to lose focus after less than thirty seconds. Our minds easily wander, and the rise in the use of smartphones and other technology is causing our ability to focus for more than a short amount of time to diminish further. All the more reason that we must carefully craft a story to grab and hold attention. If you can't capture the audience in the first paragraph or the first minute with something appetizing, they may not make it to the entrée with you.

Once you've grabbed the attention of the audience, you'll start to build out the story. Storyboarding, a visual representation of a story originated by Walt Disney Productions in the 1930s, can be a great way to outline, craft, and focus your stories. The process allows you to brainstorm ideas individually or in a group and build the story in pieces, moving the ingredients around to test what works best.

You might use, for example, post-its or index cards and a corkboard to outline the story and list the ingredients. To start, a story should include a character, a destination or goal, an obstacle, and a resolution.

One Person, Place, or Thing

Introduce a single person, place or thing. Mother Teresa said, "If I look at the mass, I will never act. If I look at the one, I will." It is human nature. We cannot wrap our heads around something we can't fathom or relate to. It becomes a statistic. Therefore, it's important to tell a story about *one person, one family, or one event*. This is commonly referred to as the identifiable victim. Focusing on an identifiable victim makes the story more palatable for the audience.

We can't relate to a hundred thousand homeless or hungry people. The problem seems insurmountable. Some scientists refer to this as a "hope gap"—the void between an overwhelming problem and the potential for solutions. We can't successfully fundraise by merely asking for help for the faceless masses. It's too difficult to create empathy under those circumstances. It's too abstract. But a food bank might highlight a particular child or family that uses its services, to inspire gifts.

Be Specific

Include *specific details* about the characters in the story to be more compelling. Give details about time and place, too. "A long time ago" could mean two years to some and twenty years to others. *Specificity* makes the story more authentic and relatable.

Rich details will ignite the sensory cortex of the brain. *The woman's name was Cindy, and she wore a cherry red velvet dress as we danced on the rooftop over the twinkling lights of the city*. Does this create a picture in your mind? That's a normal response because the brain has a natural tendency to create a visual image using the details. That's the outcome you're hoping for—that your audience will flesh out the story and create an image in their minds.

Images are potent tools. A photo or video is always more powerful than any descriptive words. It only takes a few seconds for your audience to process information from an image. In fact, an image is processed sixty thousand times faster than text. An eye-catching image can quickly pull the audience in and trigger empathy.

Infographics are a common visual tool, and they can be used to tell a great story. They can stand alone or complement another story format. You can share compelling numbers and information about the problem you're

---

Which Example Pulls at *Your* Heart Strings?

Read the following two paragraphs and think about which is more apt to tug at your heartstrings:

Story Version 1

Petey is a yellow Labrador retriever who suffered unimaginable abuse. He was found chained to a fence and abandoned in West Philadelphia. To escape, he had apparently chewed his leg, and as a result, his leg is severely infected. Before Petey can find a forever-home, he will need surgery and expensive medical attention. With a gift today, you can help to provide Petey with the medical care he needs. Can we count on your help?

Story Version 2

Dogs are the most common victims of animal abuse, accounting for 64.5 percent of all documented cruelty cases that are media reported. It's estimated that six thousand dogs are abused every year. Before 1986, there were only four states that had laws against animal cruelty. More recently, continuous chaining of a dog has become illegal in some states because owners would never let their animals off the chain during their entire lives. About half of all dogs who wind up in shelters end up being euthanized. Your gift today can help us to change these statistics.

Research studies indicate that most people will choose a scenario that looks like A. Would *you* be more inspired to donate to help Petey, or to change some statistics?

Animal abuse, homelessness, even rising college tuition can seem like issues that are impossible to resolve. If instead you focus on one single opportunity to make a difference, the story will have more impact and is more likely to generate gifts. You *can* create empathy for one person's struggle, especially when that struggle is shared in a compelling story with specific, vivid details.

working to solve, the volunteers you've engaged in the project, or the people you've impacted. An infographic can help to tell your story in a simple, easy-to-understand format.

Keep It Simple, Real, and Honest

Keep the story *simple,* as if you're sharing a story with a friend, to make it more authentic. You wouldn't use jargon or complex words if you were talking to a friend. You would use action verbs and short sentences. Your story should be written at a middle-school level. Resist the temptation to use complex sentences and words.

Similarly, be sure the story is real and honest. Ideally, allow people to tell their own stories. The next best thing is to share personal stories of real people. Be sure, of course, that you have permission to share these stories. If you must change names or use characters that aren't real, be sure to communicate that.

Tell your story honestly. Don't leave out the ugly details—in fact, the ugly details will often make the story better. Admit your shortcomings. This makes the story relatable and memorable. If you ran into a friend at a coffee shop, and she spent a few minutes talking about her neurotic family and all the issues she was dealing with, you'd probably lend a sympathetic ear. If, on the other hand, she started to tell you all about her fabulous vacations and how successful her children are, you'd probably look for the nearest exit. It's human nature.

If a story is about something that's easy or doesn't present a challenge, people don't care quite as much. We are more receptive to struggles, perhaps because we can relate. Chances are good that you have never gone home after a meeting or conference and shared presentation slides with your friends and family. But you probably *have* shared a story about a friend who is struggling. Those stories are memorable because they are simple, real, and honest.

The Hero's Journey

When you share a story, you are taking your audience on a journey. The hero's journey, or monomyth, is a universal format for storytelling that works well for nonprofit storytelling. It was described by Joseph Campbell in *The Hero with a Thousand Faces*:

> *A hero ventures forth from the world of common day into a region of supernatural wonder: fabulous forces are there encountered, and*

a decisive victory is won: the hero comes back from this mysterious adventure with the power to bestow boons on his fellow man.

Hollywood has used this format repeatedly. In fact, George Lucas credits Campbell with influencing his Star Wars series. While you might not be sharing stories of galactic proportions, you can serve up bite-sized versions of the hero's journey in your stories.

Share a Struggle

The rising action of the hero's journey to overcome an obstacle or solve a problem creates anticipation and builds tension. It might also be something unanticipated (a surprise!) that happened to the character along the way. It's the obstacle that makes things interesting.

Imagine a story about the microphone that stopped working midway through an important presentation, the car that broke down on the way to the job interview, or three teenage children who suddenly lost their parents in an automobile accident. Your audience members should be on the edge of their seats, wondering what will happen next.

A good story will give your audience a reason to stay tuned. Without a problem for the characters to solve, the story becomes boring and predictable. Why? The conflict triggers emotion. That emotion doesn't have to be sadness. The emotion might be frustration, joy, grief, despair, or any other strong emotion. In fact, if your story already has a happy ending, why would a donor want to help?

The science tells us when you share a compelling story that triggers an emotional response, the brain releases oxytocin that causes you to feel empathy. And e*mpathy* is a key ingredient for the secret sauce of storytelling that in turn triggers generosity.

Russell James, who wrote the Foreword, is a professor at Texas Tech University. He directs the on-campus and online graduate program in Charitable Financial Planning, and he has done extensive research on brain activity in fundraising and on what motivates people to make charitable gifts. His research is especially focused on what motivates major and planned gifts, and he has generously shared his findings. Just Google his name and you'll find some of his more than 150 publications in academic journals, conference proceedings, and books.

More recently, Russell has taken the well-established hero's journey concept and interpreted it as a simple command that applies to nonprofit storytelling: advance the donor hero's story. Advancing, rather than creating the donor hero story, means a charitable gift should fit within the donor's existing life narrative.

As fundraisers, we should be listening to the donor's life story and looking for ways to allow donors to be part of something bigger than themselves. Russell firmly believes if you master the command—advance the donor's hero story—you will be powerfully effective in raising annual gifts, major gifts, and legacy gifts. He admits that it's not a simple task—mastering the command represents enormous complexity.

Storytelling takes skill, practice, and artistry.

It is the artistry of storytelling that lends itself to the many variations on the recipe for great stories. In addition to the essential ingredients: a hook, characters, specific details, rich images, rising action, and a conflict that evokes empathy, there are a variety of other spices that add might flavor to your story. A story might include jokes, metaphors, contrasts, quotes, historical references, personal experiences, and more. These optional ingredients might make your story more compelling and how you add them is merely a matter of taste.

Happily Ever After

Every good story must have a resolution or transformation. It may not always be a happy ending, but it usually resolves the tension and conflict that was building. The resolution provides meaning for the journey.
This part of the story dovetails with the main objectives of nonprofits: transformation. Nonprofits exist to bring about change. When you use a compelling story to illustrate a transformation or need for a change, your donors can envision themselves as part of that transformation.

The resolution of the story must include a call to action. What response do you want from the audience? If, for example, your objective is donations, be sure your stories clearly communicate how your donors can help. Allow them to be a part of your organization's story—to be the hero. Give them options and a path forward that might include donating, sharing, volunteering, getting more involved, learning more, signing a petition, or anything else you might find helpful to your organization.

Andrew Stanton, the writer of *Toy Story* and *Finding Nemo,* explored this in his TED talk, *The Clues to a Great Story*. He shared with his audience that the greatest story commandment is: make me care. With the right ingredients in your stories, you can create and share a story that can make that happen. Now that you know what they are, turn to the next chapter for ways to gather them.

Chapter Three

Shopping for the Perfect Ingredients: Finding Your Stories

A story with a moral appended is like the bill of a mosquito. It bores you and then injects a stinging drop to irritate your conscience.

—**O. Henry**

You've planned the menu, and you have your recipes and shopping list in hand, so you set out to shop for the ingredients. You might stop at the supermarket, a bulk store like Costco, or a specialty store such as an Italian deli (they have the best fresh mozzarella!). The local farmers' market is, of course, an excellent source for the freshest produce. Perhaps you even stop in your own garden for the herbs—a little fresh basil or rosemary.

Just as you'd go to these various and assorted places for the best ingredients to prepare a gourmet meal, it's important to consider a variety of *sources* to serve up the best stories. There are plenty of places to shop for good stories if you think creatively!

Storytelling is a reciprocal relationship—there are two parts: telling and listening. In any connection, but especially with donors, the key to understanding is listening. This takes effort because we listen at a much faster pace than we speak. Too often, instead of listening, we're thinking about how we're going to reply.

In a conversation where we are gathering information, building a relationship, and seeking understanding, we should be listening more than we speak. In a donor visit, we should ideally be speaking about 30 percent of the time and listening about 70 percent of the time. Only if we truly listen can we pick up on subtle cues.

Great listening is necessary to gather and share good stories from various sources.

When you do speak, you want to use your time wisely. Ask the right questions. To determine whether someone might be a good source for a story, ask, *What does this person have to share?* Then ask follow-up questions to gather more details.

Some Questions to Ask

Questions you can ask to gather story ingredients:

- How did you start your relationship with us?
- What was your first impression of our organization?
- What surprised you when you learned more?
- What impact has your involvement with the organization had on you?
- How do you think it has impacted others?
- What are you passionate about?
- How did you feel when you made your most recent gift? (or when you volunteered?)
- How do you think your gifts make a difference?
- How would you wish to make an impact with your gifts?
- Tell me about some of the people you have volunteered/worked with.
- What would you say to a new donor or volunteer?
- What do you tell your friends about us?
- What challenges do you see for us?
- Is there anything else you'd like to share?

Ask follow-up questions, ask why, and ask for examples!

Start with Your Friends

Just as the supermarket is the obvious place to shop for food, the most obvious place to shop for stories is with your closest friends. Your loyal donors and prospects are your bread and butter. Many nonprofit organizations successfully share donor stories in the form of testimonials or donor profiles.

Similarly, shop for stories from staff or volunteers (especially long-term board members) who have worked to advance your mission and witnessed the impact. Your staff members and volunteers can be a source of stories in two ways—they can share their own personal stories of how they have been a part of the effort to advance your mission, and they can listen for stories as story shoppers. You can gather stories during a staff or board retreat or by hosting a special storytelling workshop.

A storytelling workshop is a great way to create a culture of storytelling at your organization. Train staff and volunteers to listen and share stories. Provide examples of both good and bad stories. Let them know what kind of stories you're looking for. It's difficult to predict how or when staff and volunteers might interact with people who may have stories to tell. You want your team to be equipped and ready to recognize a good story worth gathering.

There are many resources available to offer storytelling training, ranging from free online resources to consulting with a professional storytelling coach. Gathering stories can be fun. The most important thing to keep in mind is that the person collecting the story must gather enough information for someone to follow up.

A story prompt can be a useful tool to get the creative juices flowing. Offer the team opportunities to practice. Gather small groups around a table and use a timer.

Ask questions that might trigger story ideas. What have the staff answering the phones heard from callers lately? Are they hearing about problems and solutions? Are there success stories? Or are they hearing that there is significant work to be done? To gather personal stories from staff and volunteers, you might also look for stories in the research or projects your staff and volunteers are working on. How are *they* moving the needle? If they've been with you a long time, they are (hopefully!) passionate about the work they're doing and the work of your organization. Allow them to share that passion and be part of your organization's story with a prompt.

> **Let's Get the Creative Juices Flowing**
>
> Use this story prompt to craft your story:
>
> 1. Once upon a time… (set up the time and place, introduce your main character)
> 2. He/she usually… (the everyday, normal situation is explored)
> 3. But then… (the drama begins—with a conflict to resolve)
> 4. At some point… (the character starts to solve the problem)
> 5. And then… (but there are obstacles or challenges)
> 6. Until finally… (the character successfully finds a resolution)

Your board members are a special category of volunteers—as they are likely to be donors as well. Because of this, you may choose to approach them in several ways. Consider interviewing your longest-serving board members and ask them what they tell people about your organization. Don't forget your retired staff and volunteers (including retired board members). They may be happy to share stories that have been lost or forgotten over the years. They add depth and history and may even provide leads to additional stories—such as those that led to the creation of your nonprofit, your legacy society, or a key department.

It's easier, of course, to ask these questions and discover these details—the when, why, over time, and now—from living donors and volunteers. A surviving spouse or family member might be able to provide this information for a bequest or other gift.

If you have great stories, your most loyal friends will also become your storytellers. They will share and repeat the best recipes with their friends and family, becoming evangelists for your organization. This is especially true in the world of social media (more on that in **Chapter Six**).

Shop in All the Aisles

Beyond your closest friends, there are many other places to shop for stories. Be resourceful and creative. Look at all your organization's activities and programs to find places to shop for stories. Integrate your quest for stories into everything your organization is already doing.

In your mailings and emails (including annual appeals and thank you letters), look for opportunities to include a response mechanism that includes a story prompt to allow recipients to share their experiences. If your organization is event-driven, consider using a story collection form (see sample in **Appendix A**) to gather stories from attendees. At a formal event like a gala, you might offer a notebook and pen at the tables and invite stories. All of these options can, of course, also point the audience to your website where they might share stories. Surveys are another great place to gather stories.

The University of Pennsylvania recently added a new method of gathering and sharing stories: a StorySLAM. While the concept of a StorySLAM wasn't new, it was a novel concept for the School of Nursing. A StorySLAM is a live storytelling competition. The storytellers (slammers) had six minutes to share (not read) their stories grounded in the theme of innovation, which explored the breadth, depth, and diversity of nursing.

Penn faculty, students, and nursing staff were invited to submit story proposals and compete for prizes donated by a partner organization. Tickets for the event sold out, and there was a long waitlist to attend. Penn Nursing will continue to share the recorded stories in both print and video format to demonstrate the dynamic and complex role of nurses. It was, all around, a great storytelling experience.

Don't limit yourself—some stories will be long and include rich descriptions and compelling narrative. But a story doesn't have to be long to have an impact. In the chapters that follow, I'll explore the different ways you can dish up a story. For now, be open-minded as you're thinking about shopping for stories. Stories come in many flavors. Sometimes, a story can have a high impact even without words.

Perhaps one of the most unforgettable Budweiser commercials ever aired was during the 2002 Super Bowl. It was just a few months after 9/11, and the nation and the City of New York were still in pain. The commercial told a powerful story without any words at all.

The Clydesdales leave the barn and travel across the country. The action rises as they approach New York City via the Brooklyn Bridge. They arrive in Battery Park, facing the Statue of Liberty and the New York City skyline, and take a majestic and emotional bow.

The commercial aired only once. Ever. If you've never seen it, you can find it online, and it's worth watching. It was a tearjerker then, and it still is. Using only images and a somber soundtrack, the commercial made a powerful statement and told a story that would leave a lasting impact on millions of viewers across the nation.

More recently, Budweiser commercials have featured a yellow Lab puppy named, of course, "Clydesdale." In one, Clydesdale goes missing when he follows his buddy, one of the horses. As the action continues to rise, the puppy is threatened by a wolf. The team of Clydesdales comes to his rescue, and he's reunited with his owner.

Your goal is to have a solid ending. A happy ending, which makes a great resolution, is one way to do that. But the good guys don't always win, do they? A solid ending doesn't always equal a "happily ever after." Sometimes, it's a reflection, a life lesson, or a powerful statement.

Do you have examples of stories that have resonated for your organization in the past? If so, look at those stories. What characteristics do they have in common? Can you update or recreate that success with a new story?

> ### Make Sure You Have Permission to Use a Story
>
> Remember to get details and seek permissions so that you can share the stories. In **Appendix B,** you will find a sample consent form that you can adapt for your organization's story shopping purposes. If you are gathering stories electronically (such as from your website), you might want to include a link to the consent form, or a check-off box that describes the terms and conditions of sharing a story and allows the storyteller to give permission for your organization to share the story.

What do you do with all these stories you've gathered? Share them! But also save some for later—because good stories are worth repeating. Create a story cookbook, also known as a *story bank*, to include a collection of your best recipes for compelling stories for effective fundraising and communication. Create a system to note details such as dates, topics, and demographics. As your story bank grows, the system you create will make it easier to find the stories when you need them. In the next chapter, I'll talk about the entrée—using stories to engage friends and raise money.

Chapter Four

Serving up the Entrée: Sharing Your Stories

The most powerful person in the world is the storyteller.

—Steve Jobs

With the right stories, you can make the world a better place. It may sound cliché, but it's true! As a fundraiser, you already have special ingredients for stories in your kitchen that commercial entities are paying big money to try to create from scratch. Nonprofit organizations exist to make the world a better place. With stories, you can dish up your mission and inspire your audience.

It's important to make the distinction, however, between a nonprofit mission and a nonprofit story. Your mission is not your story, but it is a very special ingredient. Sharing stories in a variety of formats will bring your mission to life, add flavor, and make it real. You probably have your mission memorized and can recite it. But can you just as readily share stories that give your audience a taste of the work of your organization?

Stories will demonstrate why you are doing the work, who it involves, and who it impacts. Stories can also be used as a tool to articulate your value proposition and why you stand out from others. What are the things that make you different from other organizations?

Stories are your entrée. They blend together the delicious details of why you exist, who you serve, and how you do it. The right stories will strengthen your organization's brand and at the same time make *you* a better fundraiser and communicator.

One good place to start is at the beginning (of course!) and from the inside with your organization's origin story. Start with your *Once upon a time*. Think about the details of your founders—the people who were there at the beginning. If your founders were telling their story, would they tell you about something that triggered the *need* for your organization? Very often, you'll find something interesting there that might be your signature story. Perhaps you can capture the founder's passion, focus on your organization's purpose, and build upon the story by sharing it.

The Make-A-Wish Foundation was inspired by U.S. Customs Agent Tommy Austin. He wanted to grant the wish of Christopher, a seven-year-old boy with leukemia. Chris wished to be a police officer to "catch the bad guys." His wish was granted when he spent the day in uniform and rode in a police helicopter. Since then, the organization has granted hundreds of thousands of wishes for children with life-threatening medical conditions.

Feeding America (formerly America's Second Harvest) traces its roots to John van Hengel, the "father of food banking." He created the first food bank after meeting a mother of ten children who was rummaging for food from the discards of a grocery store. She suggested that discarded food should be saved for people to pick up just as money is saved in "banks" for future use. Today, Feeding America feeds forty-six million people at risk of hunger and is the nation's largest domestic hunger-relief organization.

And St. Jude Children's Research Hospital was started by an actor, comedian, and storyteller (yes, storyteller!). Danny Thomas made a prayerful promise to St. Jude Thaddeus, the patron saint of lost causes, during a time of despair early in his career. Founded on the belief that "no child should die in the dawn of life," St. Jude has made incredible strides in the most difficult cases of childhood cancer. When St. Jude was founded in 1962, the survival rate for childhood cancer was less than twenty percent. Today, this number stands at more than eighty percent, a complete and remarkable reversal.

All three of these organizations—Make-A-Wish, Feeding America, and St. Jude—are masterful at consistently sharing stories that are rich with images of children and families, and details that evoke emotion and motivate their audiences to support their cause. (Look for more about their success stories in **Chapter Nine**.)

Every organization has an origin story. Are you familiar with yours? Your board members should be familiar with these stories as well. Look for ways to capture these stories and demonstrate how far you've come and where you're headed next.

Just as your mission isn't your story, don't make the mistake of just listing your organization's accomplishments and calling that your story. You will be more successful if you can illustrate the impact of your organization by spotlighting the beneficiaries of your good work.

It's easy to fall into the trap of citing accomplishments and making the organization the hero. But you want to make your *donors* the heroes! You're the helper. Connect the dots from your donor's support, to your work, to the recipients of that good work.

One of the best ways to do this is to talk about the before-and-after stories of the people who have been the recipients of your organization's important mission. A good story won't just *tell* someone about it; it will *show* the impact of your mission. And in doing so, you won't just tell your donors how they can help, you'll *show* them how they can help.

The Greater Lawrence Family Health Center, a community health center in Massachusetts, tasked its college intern with creating a short publication that includes stories, pictures, and infographics. It called the publication "Storytelling our Mission" and used it to educate and motivate its staff and volunteers. The project helped to create a culture of storytelling and equipped the organization with the stories to share more about its work and effectively say, "It's more than just that."

Not content to merely *tell* people about its good work, it *showed* the impact by sharing the stories with legislators (it relies on a small amount of federal funding), donors, foundations, and the community. It repurposed the stories at its gala and on social media. It included the storytelling publication in a foundation grant application and received $100,000 to fund a mobile health unit. The feedback from the foundation indicated that the stories shared in the publication helped to differentiate its grant application. Its stories resonated.

Do Stories *Really* Take the Cake?

The experience of this nonprofit organization is not unusual. Stories will increase the effectiveness of staff and volunteers *and* enhance results. Adam M. Grant is the author of bestselling books such as *Give and Take* and *Option B* (written with Sheryl Sandberg). He's also a prolific source of wisdom and information in his blogs, tweets, and newsletters. Adam explores what motivates people and what happens when someone is a "giver" (as opposed to a taker).

I spoke with Adam about some of his studies on the impact of stories. In those studies, he wanted to find out what happens when fundraisers were not just *told* that their work was important, but instead, they met a beneficiary and heard the real story of the impact of their fundraising work.

The fundraisers in his study took a five-minute break from their fundraising calls to hear a student's story. The student, Will, was successful and charismatic. He shared a compelling story about how grateful he was for the scholarship that enabled him to afford his tuition and enjoy his time as a student at the University of Michigan.

The group of fundraisers that met Will for just five minutes increased their time on the phone in the weeks that followed by 142 percent and increased their weekly revenue from donations by 171 percent. Adam admits he dramatically underestimated the power of Will's story. In the follow-up interviews, the fundraisers admitted they were thinking of Will while on their calls. They even admitted to sharing Will's story even though they were supposed to be following a script. It was clear that giving the fundraisers a storytelling technique was highly effective.

But Adam wanted to be sure that the results of this study hadn't been skewed by Will's charisma and so they tested the fundraisers again. This time, they replaced Will with a very quiet and painfully shy student named Emily. When she shared her story with the fundraisers, she stared at her shoes and was clearly uncomfortable as she described how the scholarship was life-changing for her.

Adam expected the worst. He thought for sure that the story wouldn't have the same impact this time as it did with Will—and he was right. The Emily effect was two-and-a-half times *stronger* than the Will effect!

Anxious to understand why, Adam asked follow-up questions of the fundraisers, who deemed Emily more authentic and sincere. The fundraisers perceived that Emily deeply and genuinely appreciated her scholarship. Her story showed emotion, and it was clear the scholarship had made a huge difference for Emily. Will, they thought, might have succeeded even without the scholarship, but they wondered where Emily would be without hers. The level of perceived need and the resulting impact was much higher for Emily. Her story had clearly resonated.

The Delicious Takeaways

Fundraisers and nonprofit organizations often tell a story to remind people of why the organization's work is significant. While this can be effective, it is much more powerful to hear a story from the person who benefitted. Stories that really focus on the impact to a beneficiary will have a positive influence on both the fundraiser and the fundraising results.

The stories shared by a beneficiary are heartfelt and authentic. The stories can highlight where the recipient would be without the help of your organization, and specific details can be used to demonstrate the level of impact. The story doesn't have to be slick, scripted, or well-rehearsed. In fact, it will yield better results if it is simple, honest, and genuine. A story that is too well-orchestrated may raise suspicions, but one that is sincere, that is real, is the ideal.

To take this one step further and inspire change, remember to include stories about *potential* impact—those people yet to be served by your organization. This can be a great motivator and allows your donors to focus on dreams for the future, too. Be specific about how you will achieve your goals, including details of potential outcomes in simple terms. Show your prospects in an emotional way how their personal passions and goals match your mission.

People won't help you if they don't understand the unmet need. The stories about your potential impact can be shared in the context of a story about what you could do—how much more impact you could have if you had the resources. Don't end your story with a success that makes your audience think the problem is solved. Instead, leave them with a call to action and an opportunity to be a hero.

In the next chapter, I'll talk about the best ways to spice up your stories—especially for presentations.

Chapter Five

Variations on the Recipe: Adding Spice to Your Stories

The greatest art in the world is the art of storytelling.

—Cecil B. DeMille

Historically, all storytelling was oral. Now, we live in a world where the ever-increasing presence of technology means there is no shortage of options for storytelling. Much can be accomplished using the various formats and channels for storytelling, and the next chapter will include a taste of some of those options. In this chapter, the focus is on one of the most powerful opportunities for storytelling: sharing a story in person. The spoken word is more effective than any other method of communication.

In the 1990s, I was fundraising for the American Heart Association. At a major gifts training seminar, well-known speaker and author Jerold Panas spoke as a presenter. He shared a story that would later appear in his book, *Asking,* about a personal gift received from a client organization—a milking stool with a brass plaque on it that said, "You won't get milk from a cow by sending a letter. And you won't get milk by calling on the phone. The only way to get milk from a cow is to sit by its side and milk it."

This story and its lesson about face-to-face conversations stayed with me over the years. I have cultivated and closed gifts by letter, by phone, and even by e-mail. Donors considering significant gifts, however, often require the personal attention of a face-to-face conversation. I think the same is true of a great story—it's best told in person.

As a gift planner, I often use stories to explain complex gift options. It makes the concepts much easier to understand. Gift planning is, in part, about solving a donor's problems. When a donor says, "I'd like to give more, but...," it is a clue that a planned gift might provide a solution to the problem. You can share a story about a gift that solves that problem. And a story is one of the best ways to present a complex option (such as a complex charitable trust) in simple terms.

Recently, I worked with a donor on a significant real estate gift. He purchased his first property as a young man. He had learned from his father how to fix things and was very handy—so he bought a multifamily house that was in disrepair and needed a lot of work. He lived in the house, fixed it up, and rented it out. With the rental income, he purchased another property and repeated the process. Over several decades, he accumulated thirty-one rental units. Now, after fifty years of being a landlord, he was growing tired of the responsibility, and he was ready to retire.

He was, however, facing a tax problem. If he sold the properties, his capital gains taxes would be significant. I shared with him the story of a similar situation in which we had used a charitable trust to address the donor's tax concerns, provide an income stream, and make a significant impact with a charitable gift. He had questions, and he took some time to think it over, but he really liked the idea, and soon he was ready to move forward. Sharing a story about a gift—not the just the complex gift vehicle—allowed him to understand and relate.

In your role as a fundraiser, you have conversations with stakeholders that include, among others, prospects, donors, volunteers, board members, and colleagues. You might tell a story to one person during a face-to-face visit, ten people at a meeting, or eight hundred people at an event or conference.

The essential ingredients for stories discussed in the earlier chapters of this book—things like a beginning, middle, and end, compelling characters, conflict, and resolution—these things will remain the same. The audience members will still be the hero, and it will be their journey. Presentations, however, include a few extra special ingredients to spice things up and make them appetizing.

Too many presentations are boring and ineffective because they don't include these extra special ingredients. Think about a time that you were in the audience, and the presentation didn't go well. When a presentation is dull and flavorless, you quickly lose your appetite. You probably knew what was happening within the first few minutes.

Studies show that a speaker has about thirty seconds to grab the audience and pull them in. A good presenter will frame the presentation in a story that will hook the audience, persuade them, and inspire them to take action. They will make a connection and share a message that resonates.

In the same way that your mouth waters and your taste buds perk up when you anticipate and then taste delicious food, a good presentation will spark a physical reaction. You'll be on the edge of your seat, captivated by the message. Your heart might race, or your emotions may be aroused as your interest in where the story will end grows. The audience *wants* to connect with the speaker.

So, don't spend the first few minutes of your presentation introducing yourself and explaining what you will talk about. You only have a few minutes to make a first impression and grab the attention of your audience. You can convey the introductory information later—or even better, provide it in advance or in a handout. Use those first few minutes instead to pull your audience in with a story, a startling fact, a question, or something unusual.

Give 'em a Taste!

Once you've captured the attention of your audience with a hook, it's important to lead with a strong point or at least tease the listener with it. Give them a taste of what's to come. Don't slowly build up to your strongest point. You run the risk of losing the listener along the way.

Another way to do this is to use a storytelling technique called *in media res,* which is Latin for in the midst of things. Instead of starting at the beginning, the story jumps right into the action and then circles back to explain how you got there. You've seen this many times in literature (*Hamlet* begins after the death of his father) and in movies (in *Titanic* the ship has already sunk). This is an effective way to grab the attention of the audience and know that they will stick around to find out what happened and why.

Prepare powerful opening and closing sentences. If you have the time and inclination to memorize the entire presentation, that's certainly an option. Every presenter has a preferred method. In some cases, using an outline or notes allows for a more natural presentation. In other cases, it may be necessary to memorize your presentation.

If you're on a stage, use it to your advantage by moving around just a bit (but don't pace!) and using your hands for emphasis. Don't hide behind the podium. Similarly, don't hide behind your presentation slides by making the audience read data or bullet point filled slides. They could read them without you. In fact, if they're spending time reading your slides, your audience is not listening to you.

At Amazon, founder and CEO Jeff Bezos banned PowerPoint (or any other slide-oriented) presentations in meetings. Instead, he said, "we write narratively structured six-page memos." Bezos understands the importance of storytelling in effective communication. He said, "You can have the best technology, you can have the best business model, but if the storytelling isn't amazing, it won't matter."

If you use slides, it is far more effective to use them to *add* to your presentation with images, simple diagrams, or charts that *help* you to tell your story. The right pictures will keep the focus on your presentation. Instead of reading your slides, you want the audience to experience your presentation as if they are enjoying a delicious meal—or breaking bread—with you.

Breaking Bread

The phrase "breaking bread together" has ancient and biblical origins. While used less frequently today, it still suggests sharing an emotional experience in addition to a meal. Breaking bread and sharing stories naturally go together. Like sharing a meal together, presentations allow for human connection in a way that other formats can't.

When you are sharing a story in person, you should be sharing an emotional experience.

Smile. Make eye contact. Share a personal story about your experience with the organization and those that have benefitted. Give the audience an idea of why you care about the topic. Share something from behind the scenes about your organization such as a project or an idea that's still in the works.

If you're struggling with an issue, maybe something as real as a shortage of space in the office, share that story. You're aiming for a human connection, and that only happens during a presentation when people can relate to your story.

Great storytellers will connect with the audience by listening with all their senses and responding to things like eye contact, body language, and questions. In a face-to-face visit, you will take everything around you into consideration. Are there family photos in the room? Personal possessions that give you clues to experiences or values? One of the greatest advantages to storytelling in person is the unique ability to adjust the story to the audience in the moment.

In a meeting of several people, you might adjust your story to include members in the room who have been a part of the story. This might be a "thank you" story (for a gift or an action) or a story that recognizes the involvement and support of the team. You might invite others to share or respond to your stories.

In front of a room full of people, you will notice whether your audience is engaged, or if they are instead focused on their phones, laptops, or worse, nodding off. How can you pull the audience back in? Invite questions and participation. Engage them in your story with phrases such as "can you imagine?" or "have you ever?" or "how many of you have?" so that they can connect and relate with your message.

People have short attention spans, so it's not unusual to find that you'll need to pull them back in periodically during your presentation.

Remember that your audience may be asking "why," and your story needs to answer that question. Dig deep and share details that let the audience members reach their own conclusions.

Overall, your story should be strategically crafted to inspire and motivate the audience to take action. The audience might be skeptical, and they might resist. Maybe they think it can't be done. You want to tell a story that allows the audience to see possibilities and solutions. You want to provide a contrast between what things look like now, and what the future *could* look like. Early in the presentation, describe the status quo in a way that your audience understands. Then, contrast that situation with what could be. You might, for example, share that it's the middle of the year and your organization has missed its revenue forecast by 15 percent. But with a strong year-end, the goal of feeding hungry families in your community is within reach.

Share a story about the impact of your organization's great work and what would happen if you had the resources to do more. Paint a vivid picture with rich details of what WILL be. This is a classic storytelling technique recognized as a highly emotional and effective way to craft a persuasive presentation. It appeals to the head, but also tugs at the heart of your audience and inspires them to act.

One of the greatest examples of a presentation that used this storytelling technique is the *I Have a Dream* speech by Martin Luther King, Jr. This speech has been studied, analyzed, and memorized for more than fifty years as a legacy of oratory. It's also studied as a great example of storytelling.

On the steps of the Lincoln Memorial in August of 1963 before a crowd of a quarter million people on the National Mall and a television audience of millions, King shared a story. He spoke for just sixteen minutes, and those minutes were peppered with the extra special ingredients of a great presentation.

To start, King varied the pace of his speech, speeding up and slowing down both for emphasis and to build tension. He alluded to bible verses and popular songs that would connect with the audience. He also sprinkled the speech with quotations and metaphors to make the story relatable. He described, for example, the check that was written to the American people by the Declaration of Independence and the Constitution—a check that for black people turned out to be a "bad check."

> *In a sense, we have come to our nation's capital to cash a check. When the architects of our republic wrote the magnificent words of the Constitution and the Declaration of Independence, they were signing a promissory note to which every American was to fall heir. This note was a promise that all men, yes, black men as well as white men, would be guaranteed the unalienable rights of life, liberty, and the pursuit of happiness. It is obvious today that America has defaulted on this promissory note insofar as her citizens of color are concerned. Instead of honoring this sacred obligation, America has given the Negro people a bad check, a check which has come back marked 'insufficient funds.'*
>
> —Martin Luther King, Jr.

King used repetition to make his ideas and message more memorable for both the audience and the press. "I have a dream" and "let freedom ring" and "free at last" would become phrases that would stick forever. Still, perhaps the most important ingredient of King's story was contrast.

In her book *Resonate*, Nancy Duarte studies King's contrast of *what is* with *what could be* in great detail. His use of contrast provided the conflict for the story. The dramatic arc of the story unfolds as he described the present, the problem of how things are, and contrasts it with his vision of the future. He provided a solution of how things could be and inspired the audience to be the heroes that would make this future possible. He used rich imagery and vivid details to create pictures in the mind of the audience of what the future could look like.

King described a future when "little black boys and black girls will be able to join hands with little white boys and little white girls as sisters and brothers." The speech was full of emotion that, judging by the response, was clearly felt by the audience. He didn't just tell them, he showed them what could be. It was inspiring and moving, and it resonated because it was persuasive.

Granted, you may not use *all* the extra special ingredients in King's speech for your own story. In a face-to-face visit with a donor, you might carefully select just one or two ingredients to add to your story. You might seek the donor's advice or input to engage them in the solution. Before a larger audience at a campaign event, you might add several of the ingredients. You might poll the audience, invite questions, or seek shout-outs.

A good story will allow the audience to visualize themselves playing a role in the future. This empowers them to become the hero. At the very least, your presentation must interest and educate the audience.

Ideally, it will also persuade them and motivate them. Finish strong with a compelling call to action. Send the audience out to begin the next chapter of the story.

The action you call for from your audience could be to support your cause financially, to re-share your story to influence others, to roll up their sleeves and help, or to provide strategies and ideas for solutions. You might also describe the consequences of failing to act. What will the future look like if your organization is not successful? Send your audience out with the recipe for helping you to succeed. Finish strong by creating a picture of how great the world could look with their help.

Then, test your stories and presentations. Measure results. Practice them, tweak them, and adjust them to have the greatest impact. Finally, look for other ways to take the terrific entrée you've prepared and share it in other storytelling formats such as those described in the next chapter.

Chapter Six

The Side Dishes: The Many Ways Stories Can Be Served

As long as we are engaged in storytelling that moves the culture forward, it doesn't matter what format it is.

—Levar Burton

In the last chapter, the focus was on face-to-face storytelling. While stories are often best served orally, there are plenty of effective ways to include storytelling on your menu. Storytelling is in everyone's hands, and the variety of storytelling channels allows you to tailor the story to your audience. Stories won't be told the same way every time. Just as you share a story over pizza with friends differently than you share a story in a published article, your organization's stories should be adjusted to your audience, too.

More than most companies, Southwest Airlines recognizes the power of storytelling and tailoring the story to the audience. It has successfully created a storytelling culture among employees and has created authentic emotional connections with its customers.

A few years ago, its story campaign, "behind every seat is a story," collected and shared personal passenger stories. Its website featured a seat map of an airplane and allowed you to hover over a seat to read passenger stories about their experience with the airline. The story campaign was also featured using television, radio, digital marketing, social media, airport billboards, and more to reach the broadest possible audience.

Southwest even created a listening center where it has a team devoted to monitoring the news, checking the weather, and listening to its customers. It was listening software to pick up on key stories. Southwest is gathering and sharing stories in a wide variety of places.

Create a Storytelling Culture

Just like Southwest, every communication from your organization is part of your story. Indeed, storytelling *is* marketing, and it should, therefore, be a central part of your marketing and communications strategic plan. It should permeate your organization from the front desk to the board room. Think of it this way: would you rather have one great chef alone in your restaurant or a whole team collaborating to prepare and serve a great meal?

Each person on your team can play a different role, but storytelling should be important at every level of your organization including your staff, volunteers, CEO, and board members. Many people (including board members) are reluctant to ask for money, but will gladly tell a story. Everyone should be prepared to share stories about your mission that demonstrate your impact.

If you asked each member of your team to share a compelling story about why you exist, would they be able to do so? Is the message consistent, but personal? If properly trained, your entire team can become storytellers for your organization. Consider including storytelling at all meetings and in all publications. Make stories part of your goals, especially in your communications department. Storytelling should be part of the budget. Tell stories consistently by creating a storytelling calendar for your organization.

Then, look for a variety of storytellers and story sources to fill that calendar.

To nurture an organizational culture that encourages storytelling, train your staff and volunteers to listen for and use stories in every format possible. This storytelling training can be highly effective and worth the investment of time and resources. You increase your organization's capacity for storytelling by building a *team* of storytellers.

Collect the stories you hear in all formats (as discussed in **Chapter Three**). Start your meetings with storytelling—share, brainstorm, and prioritize what you can realistically accomplish. In **Appendix C,** you'll find a *storytelling culture assessment tool* you can adapt to assess your organization's capacity and readiness.

Storytelling Naturally

After an audit by a global marketing company, Ron Geatz, the Director of Global Content and the Chief Storyteller for The Nature Conservancy (TNC), was determined to truly create a storytelling culture within the organization. The audit of all TNC's materials, speeches, and more revealed they were not as good as they thought they were at storytelling. They were leading with facts rather than stories, the content wasn't forward-looking, and much of it was dense. The passion just wasn't coming through.

When they reflected on why this was true, organization leaders realized the organization had faced at least two obstacles to good storytelling. First, they fell into the trap of sublimating *story* to facts and figures and struggled with the emotion and personal nature of good storytelling. And second, they worked too hard to be sure that everyone was "singing from the same hymnal" or, to fit with the secret-sauce theme, following the exact same recipe. While there is some need for consistency, this didn't allow storytellers to share their own personal passions. And that made the stories far less compelling.

TNC realized they needed to increase and improve their storytelling training for staff and volunteers (including board members). Geatz worked with staff and volunteers, in some cases coaching them one-on-one, to identify a personal story about their work and to build their confidence in telling that personal story in front of a group of their peers. When someone tells him they're not a storyteller, he smiles and says, "everyone is a storyteller, you may not be a confident storyteller…yet!"

The results of the training were transformational—a more engaged, connected audience and tons of internal excitement around the power of stories. The personal stories of staff and volunteers strengthened TNC's ability to do their important work, and it created community. The results of the storytelling training were far more empowering and transformative than they had expected. The process continues with more training, building storytelling into position descriptions and annual goals, including storytelling into regular meetings, and making storytelling routine.

The Nature Conservancy is an international organization with resources to match. But the ideas can be tailored to a small nonprofit, too.

If you're with a smaller organization, you might create a team of storytellers, each with skills (existing or developed) in photography, video, journalism, or communications. Interns or volunteers can also bring skills and expertise. Penn regularly hires students as *visual storytelling interns* to gather images and stories.

A single communications (or development) staff member can serve as your storytelling point person to coordinate story collection, training, and planning for stories. This point person (or another) might also collaborate with external storytelling professionals.

A team approach to storytelling yields the best results. A single story won't resonate with everyone. So, you must appeal to different emotions by serving stories in various portions and in a variety of flavors. Segment your audience and use a variety of storytellers and channels. For some stories, you'll use a long narrative with juicy details. Other stories will be bite-sized.

There are *so many* options for storytelling. (By the time this book is printed, there will probably be something new and different!) The tried and true methods of storytelling are still valid. Share stories in your direct mail and email, including appeal letters, thank-you letters, and others. In your newsletters (print and digital) and other publications (including your annual or impact reports), don't focus only on stories about big gifts. Most people won't relate.

Pentera, Inc. focuses on solutions for marketing planned gifts. According to Claudine A. Donikian, CEO, *Pentera's* research indicates that good stories will double or even triple the average click-through rate in eNewsletters. But the wrong stories can decrease response rates. You don't want to share stories that won't resonate with people. Instead, share stories about how gifts (both big and small) impacted the beneficiaries.

Or, focus on something that makes a gift unusual. If, for example, you're a small nonprofit based on the West Coast, and you receive a gift from a donor in Texas, perhaps there's a story about why. On the other hand, a gift from your own community might be newsworthy on a local level.

Reach out to the community in which you serve with stories that raise awareness. Perhaps your local newspaper or news station would be interested in sharing your story if it's compelling. Including a story in a press release makes it much more interesting. Think about your community partners and influencers as evangelists. Again, they may not be willing to help you fundraise, but they might be able to pass your story along at public gatherings and community events. Technology has changed the definition of community because it has created *online* communities.

Technology Stirred the Pot

This certainly isn't the first time that technology has changed storytelling. Television and movies did that too. In 1917, the American Red Cross launched a campaign to raise $100 million. Just before the campaign kicked off, it released a movie, *The Spirit of the Red Cross*. The movie told the story of a Red Cross nurse, and it successfully boosted its campaign. The Red Cross used the latest technology, the silver screen, to share its story.

A few years ago, the Rockefeller Foundation commissioned a study to explore the power of digital storytelling. It convened a group of experts and thought leaders to discuss how to help nonprofit organizations use the power of storytelling. The group identified consistent gaps in how organizations "create, promote, and sustain storytelling cultures" and they recognized the significant opportunity for storytelling in the channels created by technology, especially for small nonprofit organizations.

Now, the internet and small screens have democratized storytelling. Storytelling isn't just for big shops or big budgets. Digital storytelling has become the norm. Websites that feature stories have become a best practice. If you're not sharing stories on your website already, that may be one of the best places to start to create a storytelling culture. Stories should flow effortlessly from your website and allow the audience to become immersed, to find more easily, and to connect emotionally with your organization. Remember: show them, don't tell them.

Your website can include links to download a podcast (a series of audio or video files) or a blog to explore topics and issues that are related to your mission and to regularly provide fresh stories. These tools allow you to focus on smaller issues, gifts, or achievements.

Social media (including Facebook, Twitter, Instagram, Snapchat, LinkedIn, and more) have all become important tools for sharing stories. All these channels can be used to drive your audience to your website or elsewhere for more details, more content, and of course, more stories. Instagram recently developed a tool that, like Facebook, allows users (and their followers) to direct gifts to nonprofits with a donate button. The link will go directly to the nonprofit's website donation form, and donors can find additional information and stories.

One of the greatest advantages of all these tools is the ability to use pictures and videos. A picture or video in a good story is worth far more than a thousand words. Pictures and video are more important than ever. Most social media channels provide storytelling options that allow pictures and video, and some include live streaming platforms. There is nothing like an image to capture emotion. When good stories resonate on social media, they spread.

A terrific example can be found in the story of an amazing cancer breakthrough called CAR T cell therapy (for chimeric antigen receptor T cells). Using cells from the HIV virus to infect healthy cells, they reprogram the immune system to attack the cancer cells. These infected cells become serial killer cells. On August 30, 2017, the U.S. Food and Drug Administration announced approval of the first-ever immunotherapy treatment for cancer.

After more than twenty years of pioneering research, Dr. Carl June and his team at Penn Medicine and the Children's Hospital of Philadelphia (CHOP) had successfully shifted the paradigm in cancer research.

Several patients had been successfully treated during clinical trials. Emily Whitehead was one of those patients, and in many ways, she represents the story of the revolutionary discovery. She suffered from acute lymphoblastic leukemia. Emily's cancer was resistant to chemotherapy, and she had relapsed after treatments. Her parents were told to take her home because there were no other options left. Instead, they enrolled her in Dr. June's immunotherapy clinical trial.

Emily woke up from the treatment, and there was no leukemia. She was cancer free, and she is still in remission nearly a decade later. Now came the announcement this revolutionary treatment had been approved by the FDA.

There was, of course, significant interest in the story by the various media outlets, and it spread like wildfire on social media. The excitement in the air was palpable, and the news spread so fast that the next day, Dr. Carl June walked into the thunderous applause of a flash mob gathered at Penn Medicine to celebrate the achievement. The moment was captured in the photo, at the right, by photographer Daniel Burke.

The image of the flash mob captured the emotion of the moment, and it was shared on Facebook, Instagram, and Twitter with the headline, "This is a landmark day in the fight against cancer." The various posts received thousands of likes, comments, and shares. The YouTube video created to share the story, *Fire with Fire,* has been viewed more than four million times.

Penn Flash Mob

Photo by Daniel Burke Photography

This is another great advantage of technology. It is a two-way street—you can collect and share stories and invite feedback with these channels. Your audience can communicate with you about their interests, and even share their own stories. Be sure to listen and respond to allow the audience to engage with you and become a part of the storytelling. It's all part of building relationships.

Give people the ability to share, comment, or interact!

Technology allows you to be nimble, to create and share your stories with a very broad audience and adjust the story to appeal to both broad and diverse audiences. You may mail a printed publication only to your high-end donors, but you can use your website and social media to reach a much broader audience. There, visitors can choose their own channel, "click for more," or hear a different kind of story.

Reheat Your Stories

Know your audience and tell different kinds of stories. Is the audience hungry for details, or do they just want the bottom line? Do they want to contribute to the story—and if so, can you open a channel for participation?

We have more ways to tell stories than ever before. The huge numbers of people using the various channels for consuming and sharing stories is exciting. That's the good news. The bad news is that there is also more competition than ever. Today, people are less likely to read an entire story as our attention spans and appetite for details continue to diminish. To stand out in a world of information overload, you need to pull people in with good stories. And once won't likely be enough.

Look at your stories—especially those that have resonated—and consider other ways to present them. The best return on your investment in quality images can be found by repurposing the visuals for various channels. Repurpose a story by using multiple formats and refreshing the content.

Measure the results, tweak the story, perhaps change the pictures or add comments and feedback, and then share it again. The audience may need to hear your message again in a slightly different way for it to resonate. Sometimes reheated or refashioned leftovers can be delicious! The stories or the format you've used in the past may not work. You might need a new recipe, or fresh ingredients.

New channels for storytelling continue to emerge. Just a few years ago Instagram was one of the least used channels for nonprofit storytelling. Now, Instagram has more than a billion users, and for many organizations (including Penn), Instagram stories are seeing greater results than any other channel (including the website). There are some new estimates that people, especially young people, will soon spend more time on Snapchat than they do on Instagram. While most nonprofits are using Facebook, not many are taking advantage of Snapchat. It can be a particularly great way to engage younger audiences and get people to share stories.

Penn is seeing a huge response to YouTube videos—where not all nonprofits are uploading videos. Will this be the next great thing? Or will something else come along? Change is inevitable—so be ready for new formats that will provide new opportunities.

Chapter Seven

The Kitchen Mishap: Navigating Change with Storytelling

The only reason to give a speech is to change the world.

—John F. Kennedy

Change is one of the few things that we are guaranteed in life. Similarly, there are changes we can count on in fundraising. There will always be changes in the tax laws. Income tax rates will fluctuate. The estate tax laws have changed more than thirty times since 2001. Technology, politics, and social standards are changing at lightning speed.

The economy will go through up and down cycles. Competition for charitable donations will continue to increase. And there will always be new trends and challenges in fundraising that change the environment and influence how we operate. Sometimes change means a temporary adjustment and other times changes cause a permanent shift.

But all these changes bring opportunities for conversation. One surefire way to seize the opportunities and successfully navigate change is to share your stories.

Because storytelling doesn't change. The method of dissemination may change—after all, we now have Facebook and Twitter. We have amazing websites and videos and YouTube to share our stories. Tomorrow, there will undoubtedly be something new. But the essential concept and importance of storytelling do not change. The human desire for storytelling is a constant. Storytelling is, in fact, a very effective tool to both foster *and* manage change.

There have been several times over the last few decades (and again more recently) where tax law changes have been a subject of concern for fundraisers. Will donors reduce their gifts because they are no longer motivated by a charitable income tax deduction? Will a significant estate tax exemption mean fewer estate gifts for nonprofit organizations?

Here again, storytelling can be a useful tool to manage change. Sharing stories about how donors are *responding* to tax law changes can be far more effective than a technical description of the actual changes. The changes present an opportunity to start a conversation, to invite your donors to share their concerns and their stories, and to provide options and solutions for what the future might look like.

In addition to changes triggered externally, sometimes we face internal change as well. Organizations must adapt and change. You can't get too comfortable because the world is always changing. Over time, you must adapt your strategic plan and perhaps even your mission. If you reflect on the history of your organization, there were probably seminal moments that changed your course or direction. The organization may have started down one path, and then pivoted to serve another purpose. This type of pivot may be caused by any number of changes—precipitated by, for example, demographics, economics, opportunities, or discoveries.

Storytelling is an effective way to communicate with your stakeholders, especially as you grow and change.

The story of March of Dimes provides a good example. Early in the 20th century, polio outbreaks reached pandemic proportions. This triggered fundraising campaigns that would forever change healthcare philanthropy. President Franklin Delano Roosevelt (a victim of polio himself) created the National Foundation for Infantile Paralysis in 1938 and pleaded by radio broadcast for donations to fight the disease.

The President's Birthday Bash was one of many fundraising events attended by wealthy friends and loyal supporters. At one particular event, a celebrity performer by the name of Eddie Cantor shared a story and proposed that people send dimes to the President. Times were tough as this was the Depression era, but he suggested that everyone could afford to contribute a dime. The White House was flooded with more than two-and-a-half million dimes (and other donations), as shown in the photo on the next page.

Marguerite 'Missy' Lehand, FDR's secretary, opening March of Dimes mail in 1938. (Everett Historical/Shutterstock.com.)

March of Dimes used storytelling very effectively, using a variety of channels and personalities to share its story. In 1946, March of Dimes featured five-year-old Frank Anderson and his story on a publicity poster to symbolize March of Dimes' fight against polio. Over time, the "poster child" concept expanded to include any person who is a prominent example, and it has been used very effectively by many nonprofits to generate gifts by tugging on your heartstrings.

With funding from March of Dimes, Dr. Jonas Salk developed a groundbreaking vaccine for polio that quickly changed the landscape of the disease. As a result, there was a point in time when the mission of March of Dimes (researching polio and serving victims of the disease) was no longer viable. The terrific discoveries and advances in the fight against polio triggered the need for significant change. One option was to declare victory and close its doors. Instead, it pivoted.

After the success of the Salk vaccine and significant debate about the focus and future of the organization, it pivoted to include a focus on the prevention of birth defects. Dr. Virginia Apgar, best known as the inventor of the Apgar score for assessing the health of a newborn child, worked for March of Dimes and shared stories extensively about the risks and impact of premature birth in popular magazines, newspapers, and academic publications.

When it became obvious that birth defects could be tied to the various circumstances of pregnancy, March of Dimes broadened its focus to include prenatal health. With each pivot, it shared stories to facilitate the change and continue to engage their audience. Now, as it focuses on the health of mothers and babies, it invites the community to share stories of their own experiences with prematurity, birth defects, or loss.

Evolutionary stories can illustrate where your organization was, where it is now, and where you hope to be in the future. For March of Dimes, that evolution is ongoing, and storytelling continues to play an important role. It is collecting and sharing stories (especially using video) from moms. It is sharing stories of adults who were born prematurely, to offer hope to new parents.

The president of the organization, Stacey Stewart, recently testified on Capitol Hill about maternal mortality. She told me that when she shared the story of a father who recently lost his wife and was left to raise his children as a single parent, it triggered an emotional response. The statistics about life-threatening complications during pregnancy are significant, but the story of this father and children was even more compelling.

Share Stories of the Bitter Moments Too

Seminal moments of your organization might also include such struggles or stumbles. Was there a time when your doors might have closed? A time when things didn't go as planned? Don't try to be perfect. People identify with flaws and imperfections. Embrace the struggle. Look for both the highs and the lows for your organization and focus on those transitions.

A story that shares a struggle, especially when you can also share the story of a recovery, can have a tremendous impact. It makes the story more authentic. Share the challenges your organization has faced and the progress that resulted. If you triumphed, tell that story!

As fundraisers, we must be nimble. In 2007, the University of Pennsylvania kicked off a comprehensive campaign with a goal of $3.5 billion. You know what happened just a short time later—the Great Recession hit hard. Many people wondered what would happen to our fundraising results and whether we would be able to hit that big goal.

At the peak of the recession, Penn hosted an event in New York City. Lehman Brothers and Bear Sterns were gone, and people were under a great deal of stress. In her remarks that evening, the president of the university,

Amy Gutmann, conveyed an important message: she told the room full of loyal Penn alumni that it was important to bring them together to say how much we cared, that we want to support them, and we would stay the course. She listened to their questions and concerns.

The advice we received as fundraisers at that time from John Zeller, our Vice President of Development, was to keep sharing our story, keep listening to our donors' stories, and keep asking. "Don't stay in your office—get out and meet with people where they are," John said. The conversations we had during this difficult time included more listening than ever before, but the storytelling continued, too. By the end of 2012, we exceeded the campaign goal with more than $4.3 billion raised.

Not every nonprofit fared as well during that time. Many organizations were forced to reduce operating costs and reevaluate programs. Some were forced to merge with other organizations or even close their doors. But overall, Americans increased their giving between 2006 and 2012. The nonprofits that fared well during (and after) the recession effectively used strategies such as strategic cost-cutting measures, sustained or increased fundraising, marketing, and communication efforts with a focus on personal relationships with stakeholders, and, you guessed it... good storytelling! Storytelling is effective in good times, but even more important in bad times.

Stories can be used to reframe the conversation in a time of crisis or controversy for your organization. If your organization is in the headlines for the wrong reasons, it's critical to be quick and transparent in managing the crisis. An effective storyteller will share honest and genuine stories to present the facts accurately and improve perceptions. Stories can effectively create understanding.

Even when an issue doesn't rise to the level of a crisis but is simply a misconception about your organization, stories can help to set the record straight. Ronald McDonald House Charities (RMHC) provides a good example. Its story began in Philadelphia with a gift from Eagles football player Fred Hill and a local McDonald's area operator/manager who agreed to donate proceeds from the Shamrock Shake. The idea caught on, and now Ronald McDonald House Charities provides houses, family rooms, and care mobiles to keep families together near the health care providers they need.

It is a common misconception, however, that the McDonald's Corporation or local hospitals provide all the funding. While local owner/operators might help, and the McDonald's Corporation is a mission partner, the organization relies heavily on donations from the community. The misconception about funding needs makes it more difficult for the organization to secure charitable gifts and so it uses storytelling to set the record straight.

The communications professionals for RMHC spend several hours a day focused on sharing content that engages and inspires people. The stories are about impacted families, volunteers, and donors. Their content is mostly about inspiring followers—but also about what they want them to do (a call to action). They've worked with bloggers, especially "mommy bloggers," to pass along stories of families who have experienced the benefits of RMHC. They have successfully created a culture of storytelling to clarify their funding needs and inspire charitable donations.

Similarly, a nonprofit with a big campaign goal or significant endowment might live with the common misconception by donors who believe their gift isn't really needed or won't have an impact. For an organization that receives (ever-dwindling) government funds, the perception might be that you don't need charitable gifts to cover your expenses.

State colleges and universities often hear this from potential donors. You can clear up these misconceptions with stories that powerfully demonstrate the impact of a gift. A good story will illustrate that every bit helps. It's worth repeating here—don't tell your donors, show them. Your stories must demonstrate that you are helping people, running your programs effectively, and spending money wisely.

The *Will & Grace* Effect

Storytelling can go beyond navigating change to *fostering* change. Stories in their best form have the power to change minds and change behavior by changing how people feel. There are many examples of change that was fostered by stories in books, movies, television and other mediums.

Storytelling has a unique power to move across cultures, race, ethnicity, and more. Recently, television stories have been cited as an impetus for changing how people feel and behave about many social issues. This is sometimes referred to as the *Will & Grace* effect. In 1998, the sitcom *Will & Grace* portrayed a friendship between Will, a gay man, and Grace, a straight woman, in a way that was utterly familiar and relatable to most

Americans. It helped to humanize and normalize what many may have considered "other."

Former Vice President Joe Biden was quoted as stating that *Will & Grace* had done more to advance the cause of the gay population of America than anything else. That's the power of story—it makes people think differently.

In the case of *Will & Grace*, the story demonstrated that being gay, and having a gay friend, is part of life. Stories can increase tolerance and reduce stereotyping. Studies have shown that when people, especially children, read stories that include positive images of characters that are different from themselves, they are more likely to be inclusive as a result of reading the story.

I observed precisely this kind of impact when my daughter, Katie, was in elementary school and she read the true story of Ruby Bridges.

In early 1960, Ruby was the first African American child to go to the all-white William Frantz Elementary school in New Orleans. As Katie read Ruby's story, she learned that people shouted horrible things at Ruby as she was escorted into the school. Only one teacher was willing to teach Ruby, and many parents took their children out of the classroom because Ruby was there.

People were angry and hostile—and it was unsettling to read about it. Katie couldn't understand why people responded this way. Ultimately, Ruby triumphed. It was truly a hero story and a very valuable lesson about civil rights and tolerance.

The messages conveyed by the story, including lessons about integration, leadership, bravery, racism, civil rights, compassion, and empathy were instilled in my daughter in a way that an ordinary social studies lesson never could accomplish. Stories can highlight the need for systemic change by allowing people to look at things from another's perspective. Put in the context of a story with a protagonist, a conflict, and a resolution, the message was clear, memorable, and relatable, even for a very young person.

Story has the power to change behavior. As fundraisers, you are attempting to change behavior when you are cultivating and soliciting charitable gifts. You can use the power of story to inspire charitable gifts and to engage people in support of your mission. You can use story to change the world.

Chapter Eight

Hell's Kitchen: The Inferno that Triggered a Seismic Change

Out of adversity comes opportunity.

—**Benjamin Franklin**

Unprecedented. It is a word that was perhaps overused during the global pandemic that descended upon us in 2020. The rapid spread of COVID-19 created a global health and economic crisis that tested the world. Our values were tested. Our leaders were tested. We were *all* tested. And we were *all* forced to navigate change.

In the previous chapter, we discussed navigating change with storytelling—and concluded that "you can use story to change the world." There will always be change. But the changes triggered by the pandemic, civil unrest, and political turmoil was at a pace and on a level we have never before experienced in modern times. The transformation is massive and ongoing.

The impact is global—but we are impacted differently. While we all struggle to make sense of the world and forge ahead, some were not convinced of the danger and feel invincible. Others feel far more vulnerable, anxious, and scared. At the height of the pandemic, many employees were able to work from home—while others were on the front lines with little protection.

Same Storm—Different Boats

As Damian Barr, an award-winning writer, said, "We are not all in the same boat. We are all in the same storm. Some are on super-yachts. Some have just the one oar."

Similarly, charitable organizations are impacted differently. Just as the needs and demands for services and assistance were skyrocketing, many nonprofit organizations suffered dramatically as their doors closed, revenue streams from ticket sales to elective surgeries were cut off, and budgets and staff were slashed.

For nonprofits that already had cash-flow issues, these difficulties were only exacerbated by the pandemic. Some charities were in real trouble; others were simply looking for the best path forward.

Early in the pandemic, many nonprofit organizations paused their fundraising efforts. They were faced with the challenge of continuing to move forward *while* being respectful of the urgency and gravity of the pandemic, particularly when asking for gifts to support anything other than coronavirus resources.

Unfortunately, some organizations retreated from fundraising due to a lack of resources or misplaced pessimism. Others paused only briefly and then thoughtfully and carefully continued to engage audiences and cultivate, solicit, and steward their donors.

In many cases, these organizations showed extraordinary resilience in the face of challenge. They continued to function and successfully pivoted to virtual programming to fundraise and engage donors and constituents. Organizations that were nimble and innovative survived, and in some cases even thrived.

Many organizations, particularly those closely connected to the virus, were the recipients of significant gifts in response to the need. People wanted to help, to be part of the solution—to *do* something! They were stuck at home and, in many cases, feeling helpless. So, they provided food and supplies for healthcare and other frontline workers, and financial support for developing treatments and vaccines.

According to research by the Indiana University Lilly Family School of Philanthropy, more than half the households in the United States gave to organizations *in some way* in the early response to the pandemic—and most households maintained their giving levels. As we moved past the early months of the crisis, giving increased.

At Penn, when the pandemic sent us home in March 2020, we were in the final fifteen months of an ambitious campaign. The goal of the Power of Penn campaign was to raise $4.1 billion in four years—and the end date was

June 30, 2021. We paused our fundraising efforts briefly and then cautiously and carefully persevered.

The gifts Penn received in response to the needs triggered by the pandemic were significant—but it was also critical that we refocus our efforts on the campaign priorities. We pivoted. Plans were modified. Events were virtual. In some cases, we reached people we had never reached before despite working exclusively from home. Donor conversations continued, and gifts closed. The campaign was ultimately successful. We broke fundraising records and exceeded the campaign goal by more than $1 billion.

Despite early concerns that pandemic-induced economic hardship would suppress philanthropy, many charities benefited from gifts of all sizes from people in a broad array of income levels. High-net-worth individuals contributed vast amounts for the pandemic but giving was not limited to resources for the pandemic.

Racial and social justice giving, for example, boomed in 2020. Donors from all backgrounds turned their attention to increasing calls for racial equity. We witnessed an outpouring of donations from individuals, corporations, and foundations that began to grow as soon as protests and other activities supporting racial and social justice spread across the country.

The events of 2020 only served to increase the importance of storytelling for successful fundraising. Andy Goodman is a storytelling guru and the Director of the Goodman Center. "Storytelling is the single most powerful communications tool available to us, period," he said.

Storytelling has been the most powerful tool forever. A global crisis won't diminish the role of storytelling. It will only *accentuate* its power.

In fact, Andy pointed out to me that during the global crisis, while other programs were cut, the Bank of America Charitable Foundation continued to fund storytelling training as part of its Neighborhood Builders Program because it was deemed so important.

The most successful organizations in the country used storytelling effectively as they navigated the path forward—and will continue to do so post-pandemic.

While we might readily recognize the benefits of storytelling for *external* audiences such as donors and prospects, it's also important to remember the advantages of using storytelling for *internal* audiences, including board members and staff, as well.

During a crisis such as an economic downturn, a natural disaster, social unrest, or a pandemic, it's easy to fall into the trap of retreating from fundraising efforts—including donor conversations and solicitations. But it is critical during these times to continue to reach out to our donors. Listening to our stakeholders becomes even more vital during a crisis. To meet the needs of our constituents, we must hear them, empathize with them, and respond to them.

Keep in Touch! Love You!

The pandemic heightened our awareness of our own mortality. Google searches related to "wills" reached an all-time high, and estate planning attorneys were very busy. The pandemic also emphasized the need to say "I love you" and "I appreciate you." This is true for family and friends—and it's especially true for our donors. We must reach out to those closest to us during difficult times, even if only to express our appreciation, concern, and support.

Sharing stories with internal audiences (such a fundraising staff or volunteers) is a great way to demonstrate how donor conversations can and should continue. Stories can offer a way to acknowledge a concern—an illness, an economic downturn, a family situation—and still move the conversation forward. You might, for example, say something like, "I understand. Other donors are feeling like you do."

The Nature Conservancy (TNC) continued to focus on storytelling skills as part of its organization-wide staff training during the pandemic. They shared the faces of donors who are *still* giving and donors who understood the importance of a connection to nature, *especially* during the lock-down period of a pandemic. Despite the pandemic, donors *increased* their giving, whether making planned gifts, outright gifts, or blended gifts.

Ed Cadogan is the Senior Regional Gift Strategist with TNC. He believes that stories are one of the best tools for training and coaching. Stories allow us to take something from an idea or a concept (such as a gift of real estate or complex asset) to a shared experience. He likes to invite major gift officers to share their stories of collaboration, thereby highlighting their accomplishments and creating an incentive for peers.

Ed enjoys sharing the "Sally Story" internally with major gift officers and board members to help raise awareness about how recent tax law changes can provide donors with an opportunity to think strategically about charitable giving. The "Sally Story" provides a great example of why it is so important *not* to assume your donors will alter their approach to giving simply because times are tough.

The Sally Story

Sally gives generous gifts to TNC of $1 million annually to save rainforests around the world. When the S&P 500 Index dived 34 percent in March 2020, many of us were uncertain how donors would respond to the pandemic-driven economic downturn. The CARES ACT passed in March 2020 allowed donors like Sally to deduct cash contributions up to 100 percent of their adjusted gross income (AGI). Sally worked closely with her CPA to reconsider her approach to giving that year, donating $2.5 million by bundling her annual gifts earmarked for future years and making them in 2020 to take advantage of the higher AGI limit.

In Ed's nearly twenty-seven years working in charitable gift planning, this may be the most attractive charitable tax provision ever for cash gifts. It helped change the way donors thought about charitable giving during the pandemic.

Remember Sally—and think big!

There are many other examples of organizations that have used storytelling effectively during a crisis. John Glier of the global consulting firm Grenzebach Glier and Associates shared several with me. He has served as an advisor to arts, voluntary, higher education, and other nonprofit organizations worldwide, including those with some of the largest fundraising campaigns.

When I asked John about organizations he observed using storytelling effectively during the global crisis, he mentioned the American Heart Association and Sloan Kettering. He also described a gift conversation with Rush University Medical Center (in Chicago) that continued despite the pandemic.

While the focus on health equity disparity wasn't new to Rush, the disproportionate COVID-19 case and mortality rates in people of color and the murder of George Floyd, and the subsequent civil unrest, thrust the issue of racial health inequities to the fore.

64 Chapter Eight ••

To tell the story in vivid detail and illustrate the stark life expectancy gap between high- and low-income neighborhoods, Rush depicted the significant gap in its primary service area along the tracks of the elevated transportation system known as the Chicago "L." With just a few train stops, life expectancy drops by more than a decade.

John described how critical it is to frame a story in the right way to the right people. A story needs to educate first—by sharing information and creating awareness—and then to inspire. A donor's motivation to give is often deeply rooted, and a powerful story can reach those roots.

In May of 2021, Rush announced a gift of $10 million from BMO Financial Group to create the Rush BMO Institute for Health Equity. The donation will provide critical support to decrease health disparities and improve health outcomes in the communities Rush serves.

Rush leaders didn't suspend donor conversations during the pandemic—they continued to tell their stories!

John also shared the experience of the Dana-Farber Cancer Institute, which launched a $2 billion campaign with a virtual kickoff event attended by more than a thousand people. The event featured legendary journalist, author, and cancer survivor Tom Brokaw as a storyteller. It featured the stories of an adult nursing student from Trinidad, a talented young singer, and a real estate developer—all cancer survivors who demonstrated impact and illustrated the strategic priorities to be supported by the campaign.

The stories showed in very real terms where Dana-Farber is now—and where it *can be* in the fight against cancer if the campaign is successful.

Storytelling allows us to bring the power of human connection to life—even through a virtual experience. As we progress in this new normal, be sure you have the tools and technology in place to be agile and creative.

Despite the pandemic, the *reason* your organization exists (the why you do what you do) probably didn't change. But *how* you do it might look different now—and some of those changes will stick.

If you didn't use technology for fundraising purposes before 2020, you're probably using it now. Virtual events and donor visits will likely continue well into the future as donors want to save travel time, increase convenience, and conserve organizational resources. Virtual content allows us new opportunities to connect with people in new ways.

The pandemic accelerated the pace of online giving and triggered a digital transformation that would have taken years. Those who were resistant or considered themselves "old school" had no choice but to learn quickly.

Video calls climbed sharply, touchless and electronic transactions became common, and the use of QR codes shot up as we replaced things like paper menus. Digital consumption is at an all-time high. Communications strategies have adjusted as we've moved beyond familiar forms.

Building Resilience

The Charities Aid Foundation America (CAF America) partnered with the Indiana University Lilly Family School of Philanthropy at IUPUI and The Resource Alliance to publish a multi-volume report highlighting the priorities that charities consider essential to their success now and for the future. The key findings of the report, entitled "Future-Proofing Nonprofits for the Post-Pandemic World," indicate that digital fundraising capabilities and communication skills will be crucial for nonprofits to remain resilient and build capacity.

The research polled charitable organizations worldwide to learn about the skillsets they relied on to sustain their operations through the crisis and the skillsets they must develop to emerge stronger.

Although a large majority of those polled indicated they have a communications plan in place, nearly as many indicated they want to learn how to communicate more effectively for fundraising and need guidance in impactful storytelling to achieve their objectives.

When I asked Ted Hart, the President and CEO of CAF America, what prompted the researchers to include a question about storytelling, he said, "We didn't! It happened organically. The charities indicated an interest in storytelling without our prompting."

The need for storytelling has never been greater—because storytelling helps us make sense of the world.

The pandemic made it very clear that we are all hungry for human connection and community. Stories can be a great way to give people—particularly your donors and other stakeholders—what they crave. In many cases, you will need to adapt your stories. What's appropriate now, what resonates now, might be very different than what worked before. The world has changed.

So, test your stories. Ask others to read and respond to them—indicating how the stories make them *feel*. What emotions does the story trigger?

That is not to say that you should abandon what's worked well in the past. Think about how many people spent time during the pandemic watching old movies or binge-watching old television shows. We find comfort in the familiar.

If you have a story that has resonated with your donors in the past, consider sharing it again. I've heard about organizations that have used the same appeal letter, containing the same story, for decades. If it works well, use it again!

But remember that this is not the time to simply return to the old ways of doing things. We can't go back. We've changed. Many of the issues of 2020 will remain unresolved for quite some time. The stories we share will extend well into the future. What do you want people to know—to remember—about you? Was your organization nimble? Resilient? Responsive? Successful?

Your donors have a role to play in how your stories continue and how they end because if you allow them to be part of the story, they may influence and determine the path forward in how *they* respond.

As with any crisis, time will tell. When we look back, we will have a better perspective on how we responded, how we pivoted, what we learned, and how we grew as a result. We will have many stories to tell. Hopefully, we will be better prepared to confront the next crisis and wave of change. There will always be changes. Keep those storytelling skills in your toolbox!

Food for Storytelling Thought

- The pandemic and other events created new stories to share. How are you capturing them?
- What stories do you want to be repeated?
- What have we learned from the crisis experiences?
- How did your donors step up and help during 2020?
- How did the global crisis impact/change your programs? Your budget?
- What will we keep as we move beyond the pandemic (e.g., virtual events and visits, impact stories)?
- How has your strategic plan changed (including goals and fundraising priorities)?
- How has your organization's vision of the future transformed?
- What will be different for your organization going forward?
- In a world filled with many big problems, how is your organization relevant?
- Has your organization's relevancy increased or decreased?

Chapter Nine

The Dessert: Sweet Success Stories

That is what storytellers do. We restore order with imagination. We instill hope again and again.

—**Walt Disney**

For many people (myself included), dessert is one of the best parts of the meal. There's something special about sweet berries and cream, chocolate chip cookies, or a decadent cannoli. If you believe that life is too short, and you should eat dessert first, maybe you skipped ahead to this chapter. If, on the other hand, you worked your way through the book to get to this point, I hope you've enjoyed the meal and that you've "saved room" for a few sweet success stories of good storytelling.

As I looked for success stories, time and time again charity: water was cited as a great example of an organization that has mastered the art of storytelling. Some have described it as the "gold standard" of nonprofit storytelling. The mission of charity: water is to bring clean and safe drinking water to people in developing nations. The organization was launched in 2006 and has already raised more than $300 million.

Scott Harrison, the founder of charity: water, is often described as its chief storyteller. He believes that nonprofit branding and marketing shouldn't be any different or less important than they are for a for-profit business. He understands the significant value of pictures and videos to convey the story in a way that words can't. In fact, when Harrison gives a presentation about the work of the organization, he uses more than two hundred photos and videos in an hour. He is a huge fan of storytelling the *right* way. Harrison explains, "I think a lot of organizations, companies, and nonprofits make themselves the hero: 'We are feeding the world. Look how great we are.' And I think charity: water has always said, 'Look how great *you* are. *You* care; *you're* giving money. *You're* giving time, and *you're* making this possible." The storytelling culture at charity: water clearly comes from the top.

Stories Are Free

You might be tempted to look at charity: water and think you don't have the marketing budget to share stories the way it does. But it *doesn't have* a marketing budget. It doesn't pay for advertising. Stories are free, and good stories will spread.

Andy Goodman has focused on storytelling and worked with charitable organizations for more than two decades. His mission is to help good causes reach more people with more impact. When I asked him what he tells the leaders of smaller organizations who want their organizations to be more effective storytellers, he said, "You don't need expensive video to tell stories, you need a team of good storytellers!"

The people on the charity: water team *are* great storytellers. They rely on people and companies to share their stories by creating partnerships. In everything they do, they share compelling stories about the impact of bringing clean water to people. Its website devotes significant space to stories. It uses stories in its email and its blog. It uses eye-catching images in all its stories, especially stories on social media and the internet. It doesn't just talk about success. Its stories *demonstrate* success.

In just one example, it presents the image of a woman who says, "I feel beautiful for the first time." The headline leaves your wondering…why didn't she feel beautiful before? And why does she feel beautiful now? As you read her story, you learn that her daily routine would include hiking to a river for water that would provide enough to cook and clean—but there was never enough water left to bathe. The average woman in Africa—and it's usually the women, not the men—walks three miles every day for water.

Now that charity: water has provided her village with a well, she finally has water to cook, to water her garden, to wash her children's clothes, and to bathe. And so, she feels beautiful for the first time. The story triggers emotion as you contemplate what it must feel like to not have enough water with which to bathe. This kind of impact on a single person is an excellent example of charity: water's extraordinary storytelling.

Twice a year, nearly six hundred donors and scholarship recipients gather to celebrate the transformative power of financial aid at the University of Pennsylvania. Scholarship students come to Penn from all over the world: a Native American student from a reservation in Florida, a homeless student from Texas, and a student from a place "Google could not name." They share stories of where they were, and where they are now. "My village knows no paved roads, police stations, or clinics. We are invisible, appearing on no maps, in a place that Google could not name," said a student from Swaziland.

"Your gift is not tuition," he told the audience. "It is being seen. I have stood an equal among my peers. I have worked with the greatest minds, led incredible teams, and have dreamt of things for mother I can't even translate into SiSwati." The students' stories are personal, real, and emotional. They include stories of unlocked potential, of the power of education, and of the impact of scholarship. The student finished his remarks by saying, "You have given me a passport to sit at tables that had never set a place for my kind. We are the bright sons and daughters of Penn."

It's not unusual for donors to enjoy the scholarship celebration, and then increase their scholarship support, according to John Zeller, Penn's Senior Vice President of Development. Now that's sweet!

In other cases of "sweet success," organizations stepped up their storytelling efforts in response to an audit of their marketing and communications strategies. Some realized they were well known but not well understood. This translated into falling short of their fundraising potential. Acquiring donors and engaging audiences was tough and retaining them was even tougher. The expert advice they received was to focus more on storytelling.

After just such an audit, the Make-A-Wish Foundation realized it had been telling the wrong story. Most people recognized Make-A-Wish and knew it granted children's wishes. Too many people didn't understand, however, that the organization granted wishes of children who were *chronically or critically* ill, not just *terminally* ill, and people didn't understand the impact of granting those wishes. Granting wishes doesn't just make a child happy for a day or a week. According to research studies, it improves a child's health status, makes them more compliant to medical orders, enhances their state of mind, increases hope and confidence in both the child and their family, and strengthens communities. Sharing stories that demonstrate that kind of impact can be incredibly compelling.

Make-A-Wish also shifted the focus from the organization as the hero, to stories that made the volunteers and donors the hero. The organization is volunteer driven. It grants fifteen thousand wishes a year, and each wish requires the work of two volunteers. So, it was important to feature the hero stories of the volunteers. The call to action of the stories is for increased donations, volunteer engagement, and medical referrals for wishes.

While it can be difficult to measure the full impact of the storytelling shift, in A/B testing, results showed a 30 percent improvement in fundraising results, according to Jono Smith, Director of Brand Communication and Digital. He shared that the shift in storytelling also had unintended consequences: it refreshed its brand identity. It allowed it to take bigger steps with its stories. It used digital technology and social media to share its stories and increased the use of photos and video to *show* its audience, rather than *tell* it, about the impact of its work.

In just one of many Make-A-Wish videos, Isaiah shares his story of the wish he was granted. He was about twelve years old at the time, his family didn't have much, and he was suffering from a chronic illness. "I'd recently seen the movie *Catwoman*," he said, "and I wanted to meet her." He didn't know that Halle Berry was Catwoman until he spent a day with her on Santa Monica Pier enjoying the rides. Isaiah said, "We had a blast, and at the end of the day, she told me to email her." Unfortunately, he revealed, his family didn't own a computer. By the time Isaiah arrived home, an Apple computer and printer had arrived on his doorstep.

The wish was life-changing. The day with Halle gave Isaiah hope and confidence. With the computer, he was able to read and learn about things he never knew existed, and it helped him to complete his schoolwork. He is now twenty-five years old, was the first in his family to graduate college (where he majored in economics and pre-med) and hopes to be a doctor someday. Isaiah is thriving, and his story could not be more effective at clearing up any misconception about the impact of the wishes made possible by Make-A-Wish donors and volunteers, including wishes granted to those who are not *terminally* ill. This story was a message of hope and inspiration. Isaiah was clearly grateful for his experience, and stories like his can resonate with your audience.

While Make-A-Wish responded to external advice about storytelling, sometimes self-reflection can yield similar results. St. Jude has long been recognized for its great storytelling. But changes in the way people connect and hear stories triggered what they believed was the need for a change. The organization realized there were limits to traditional media, and they knew they had a tremendous source of stories that unfold every day.

As a result, St. Jude recently launched a new digital storytelling platform called *St. Jude Inspire*. This new "sharable storytelling platform" is designed to build on St. Jude's ability to inspire and engage people by reaching new, diverse, and younger audiences. St. Jude has built a culture of storytelling. Story ideas will, therefore, come from staff, volunteers, patients, families, scientists, donors, and celebrities. The stories are full of pictures and videos that demonstrate the impact of its work. The program is new, but it has already established plans to measure success by evaluating how many new people are reached and engaged, which stories resonate, and whether the stories stimulate an increase in donations and volunteers.

Measure Success

It's important to measure the success of your stories by looking at things like page views, shares, comments, sign-ups, feedback, and requests for more information. Focus groups can be particularly useful for this. Measuring success is the only way your organization will know if you're telling the *right* kind of stories. "The process of systematically evaluating story success becomes critically important when thinking about reinforcing an organization-wide mindset and appreciation for stories," says Ron Geatz of TNC. "Nonprofits should look for opportunities to highlight the outcomes (anecdotal or quantitative) of shared stories and how they helped achieve measurable goals, and even build this reporting into meetings where the staff share stories."

Be prepared for the responses to your stories. Measuring success by the dollars raised is important, but measuring engagement is even more critical. If people are engaged, they will *understand,* and the dollars will follow. Two organizations providing terrific examples of increasing engagement are StoryCorps and Humans of New York.

StoryCorps was founded in 2003 with a single Storybooth in Grand Central Terminal in New York City to gather the audio stories of "everyday Americans, one story at a time." Over time, it added Storybooths, including two mobile booths that crisscross the country, to gather stories. The stories are preserved in its archive in the Library of Congress and shared via a variety of channels including radio (National Public Radio is a partner), television, books, and online social media channels. StoryCorps says:

We do this to remind one another of our shared humanity, to strengthen and build the connections between people, to teach the value of listening, and to weave into the fabric of our culture the understanding that everyone's story matters. At the same time, we are creating an invaluable archive for future generations.

The stories, framed in the form of an interview, capture highly personal and precious narrative. Some capture more ordinary experiences, and some, such as the stories that honor the lives of the victims of the 9/11 terror attacks, are extraordinary. The stories consistently evoke emotions, even tears. As a result, the stories have humanized issues, fostered connection, and increased understanding and empathy.

A few years ago, StoryCorps harnessed technology and launched an app for collecting stories—an app it referred to as "a new tool for collecting the wisdom of humanity." The app has been downloaded more than a million times. The level of engagement is huge. StoryCorps is a nonprofit organization and has partnered with a broad range of other nonprofits to gather and share stories, and to raise funds and awareness.

For example, the Juneau Public Library, a smaller nonprofit, partnered with StoryCorps to build a program highlighting stories that are often absent from the historical record, with a particular focus on the experiences of Alaskan Natives.

Another example: The American Red Cross, a well-established national organization, partnered with StoryCorps to gather stories from people whose lives have been affected by the Red Cross.

Humans of New York (HONY) isn't a nonprofit organization, but it shares some similarities with StoryCorps. The movement started in 2010 as a personal photography project by Brandon Stanton in New York City. He found himself unemployed and with a camera, so he began taking photos of people. Brandon soon added "storyteller" to his photographer role when he paired short stories with the pictures. The concept spread throughout the country and the world with a partnership with the United Nations.

The stories have inspired two bestselling books, and millions of people follow HONY on social media channels, including Facebook and Instagram. By sharing their stories, HONY has bettered the lives of countless individuals, giving them hope, encouragement, support, funding, or merely a voice. And here's the nonprofit connection: HONY has leveraged its amazing success by partnering with nonprofit organizations to raise millions of dollars for disaster relief, pediatric cancer research, and more.

Nonprofits that are successful storytellers create a culture of storytelling within their organization. They hone the skill and partner with others. They adjust and perfect their recipes. They collect stories and shore up their pantry with stories ready to serve in a variety of delicious ways. They take advantage of *every* storytelling opportunity.

Chapter Ten

Check Please! Summary and Additional Resources

I believe in the power of storytelling. Stories open our hearts to a new place, which opens our minds, which often leads to action.

—**Melinda Gates**

You are already a storyteller. You were born with the skill. Children create and share stories naturally. If I asked you to tell me a story about your family, surely you'd share something funny, or endearing, or special. What stories come to mind when you think about your mom, or your dad, or your siblings? If you're a parent, stories about your children roll easily off your tongue. Under those circumstances, storytelling comes as easily as boiling water. But it doesn't always go quite as smoothly when we try to use those skills effectively in our work to serve a gourmet meal kind of story.

As fundraisers, we understand the importance of sharing the stories of our organizations—with our missions as a focus. Sometimes, however, we fall into the trap of sharing only numbers and data. This may be a consequence of living in a data-driven world where our success is measured in numbers. How much money did you raise? What are your administrative expenses? How many people did you feed? It's easy to understand how we might become so focused on the data. But we must remember: stories trump data. While facts are an important complement to any story, it is far more memorable, persuasive, and effective to share stories than to share just facts. Becoming a *strategic* storyteller takes practice. It takes an investment of time and effort.

> **Recipe for Storytelling Secret Sauce**
>
> 1. Keep this recipe for Storytelling Secret Sauce at hand:
> 2. Start with something to capture attention (an appetizer!)
> 3. Focus on one person, place, or thing (one bite at a time)
> 4. Include images and rich, specific details whenever possible (fresh ingredients)
> 5. Keep it simple—no jargon (ingredients people don't have on hand)
> 6. Share a struggle (it makes it more palatable)
> 7. Give donors a reason to care and make *them* the hero (your celebrity chef)
> 8. Gather stories everywhere (shop in all the aisles)
> 9. Create a culture of storytelling (make it a team effort in the kitchen)
> 10. Add stories to all presentations—otherwise, it's too bland (spice things up)
> 11. Navigate change with stories (salt to taste)
> 12. Sprinkle stories liberally using all available channels (serve and reheat)
> 13. Don't forget a resolution and call to action (check please!)
> 14. Measure and celebrate results (eat dessert!)

A Good Investment!

The University of Pennsylvania and many other institutions offer storytelling courses on the liberal arts side of campus, *and* on the business side too. Courses are offered to both Wharton undergraduate students and Wharton MBAs. Storytelling has clearly become an essential skill as the business world has realized that facts tell, but stories *sell*.

Storytellers rise further in their careers. This valuable skill is recognized as important for leaders, entrepreneurs, and yes, fundraisers.

If it's not already on there, it's time to add storytelling to *your* resume.

Not only will it help your career, but it might also make you happier! According to research presented in *The Wall Street Journal*, storytellers are "happier in life and love." People who share stories in a positive way are more satisfied with their lives. What's even more interesting, storytelling is good for relationships. The same research indicates women find men who are good storytellers more attractive and desirable as long-term partners. Psychologists believe this is because storytellers demonstrate that they know how to connect and share emotion. Storytellers are more articulate and more interesting.

Andrew Stanton wrote three *Toy Story* movies. He says that storytelling is joke telling. "It's knowing your punchline, your ending, knowing that everything you're saying from the first sentence to the last is leading to a singular goal—and ideally confirming some truth that deepens our understanding of who we are as human beings." If you think about it, the best comedians tell stories. The jokes we find the funniest are the ones that we can identify with. We see ourselves, our children, our friends, or our families in those stories.

I met my husband, Mark, in law school. We shared several classes during the first two years of law school, and I knew he was a serious student and a class leader. In late September of our third and final year, there was a talent show on a Friday night in the student pub. My friend, Susan, convinced me to sing a duet with her.

Mark's friends convinced him to do a stand-up comedy routine. What a pleasant surprise it was to see a smart and attractive classmate who was also *really funny!* He told stories of his quirky Italian family that could have been from an episode of a sitcom like *Everyone Loves Raymond*. So...a few days later, I approached him and invited him to go to a comedy show with me. And the rest, as they say, is history. Mark has been making me laugh and telling me stories for more than thirty years. I knew he was funny. What I didn't understand that night in the student pub was how powerful storytelling can be.

Over time, I've learned that stories are ubiquitous. They are fun and entertaining. Stories capture the joy of living a life full of rich experiences, and I've recognized for a long time that stories are useful in my work as a fundraiser. Gathering stories in face-to-face visits with donors and prospects is one of the best parts about my chosen profession. But it took the painful experience of losing my brother for me to learn just how vital storytelling truly is, and to recognize that stories are *indeed* a way to leave a legacy.

The filmmaker Peter Gruber said, "In any situation that calls for you to persuade, convince, or manage someone or a group of people to do something, the ability to tell a purposeful story will be your secret sauce." I couldn't agree more! I hope you'll discover that reading this book provides you with food for thought. Your personal and professional experiences will shape your stories. What delicious stories will you tell?

I'd love to hear about *your* storytelling success! If you have created a culture of storytelling and told stories to increase engagement, improve fundraising results, or have a greater impact on those you serve, please let me know. If you have an entertaining story to share, I will welcome hearing about it.

Appendix A

Story Collection Form

[See next page]

Story Collection Form

Story Listener name (if applicable): _____

Storyteller name: _____

How did you learn about our organization? _____
_____
_____

What's kept you engaged? _____
_____

How has our organization impacted you? _____
_____
_____
_____

Would you be willing to share more details with us? _____

Would you be willing to share your story with others? _____

Is there something you wish our organization could do? _____
_____
_____

Contact information:

Phone _____ E-mail _____
Address _____

Appendix B

Sample Consent Form

[See next page]

Consent Form

I, _____, agree to be interviewed, filmed, audiotaped, and/or have my pictures taken. I agree that any interview information, video, audio, or photograph ("materials") can be used in publications, presentations, websites, advertising, or other media. I understand that these materials are to advance [INSERT ORGANIZATION]'s mission.

I understand and agree that [INSERT ORGANIZATION] may edit, use, publish, distribute, and republish any materials. I understand that I have no rights in the materials and I waive all right to inspect or approve the uses of materials, now or in the future.

I understand that I will not be compensated for participating in sharing my story or for the use of the materials.

I release [INSERT ORGANIZATION] and its agents, employees, and contractors from all claims, demands, and liabilities in connection with the above.

My signature below means that:

- I have read and understand this consent form.
- I have been given all of the information I asked for regarding sharing my story.
- My questions have been answered.
- I agree to everything explained above.

Printed name of the subject: _____

Signature: _____

Street: _____

City: _____ State: _____ Zip: _____

Phone number: _____ Date: _____

IF THE SUBJECT IS UNABLE TO CONSENT FOR HIMSELF/HERSELF (as identified above):

Legally responsible person: _____

Relationship to subject: _____

Signature: _____

Street: _____

City: _____ State: _____ Zip: _____

Phone number: _____ Date: _____

Appendix C

Storytelling Culture Assessment Form

[See next page]

Storytelling Culture Self-Assessment Tool

Use this worksheet to identify and rate key areas of success as well as those that need improvement in your organization's storytelling culture and readiness.

MINDSET/APPRECIATION

	🙂	😐	🙁
Belief in the value of storytelling and support for its use is uniform throughout the organization, from top to bottom.			
Staff are encouraged to share stories internally and externally.			
Staff feel confident in their abilities to share stories that illustrate the organization's mission.			
Stories are in alignment with the mission and collectively create a cohesive picture of the organization.			
Stories are regularly incorporated into a majority of organizational communications, whether spoken, in print or digitally.			
When stories are successful in leading to increased awareness, funds, etc., these successes are shared internally with staff.			
Staff are regularly encouraged to develop their storytelling skills through professional development and/or adoption of new technology.			
Planning to collect and share stories is incorporated into organization and communication/development goals.			
TOTALS			

BIT.LY/NONPROFITSTORYTELLING
#STORIESWORTHTELLING

GEORGETOWN UNIVERSITY
School of Continuing Studies

Meyer Foundation

Storytelling Culture Self-Assessment Tool

CAPACITY

	😊	😐	☹️
Staff meets at regular intervals (weekly, monthly) to share and discuss stories.			
Storytelling is incorporated into at least one staff member's core job duties.			
The staff member(s) tasked with storytelling possess necessary skills in writing, editing, production and/or visuals and video (if applicable).			
Staff storytellers seek out professional development opportunities to expand their skills when necessary.			
There is a dedicated amount within the annual communications budget for producing stories (including upkeep of software/hardware or retaining external support).			
There is an organized system for storing collected assets and completed stories in a way that allows staff to easily access them.			
If collection and production are handled by different departments/staff, there is an organized system for transferring this information from one to the other.			
Effort is made to track the impact of storytelling, as a way to enable more sustainable investment.			
TOTALS			

BIT.LY/NONPROFITSTORYTELLING
#STORIESWORTHTELLING

GEORGETOWN UNIVERSITY
School of Continuing Studies

Meyer Foundation

Courtesy of Myer Foundation

Appendix D

Resources

Books and Published Papers

Campbell, Joseph, *The Hero with a Thousand Faces, Third edition,* New World Library, 2008.

Campbell, Julia. *Storytelling in the Digital Age: A Guide for Nonprofits.* CharityChannel Press, 2017.

Cron, Lisa. *Wired for Story: The Writer's Guide to Using Brain Science to Hook Readers from the Very First Sentence.* Ten Speed Press, 2012.

Duarte, Nancy. *Resonate, Present Visual Stories that Transform Audiences.* John Wiley and Sons, 2010.

Gottschall, Jonathan. *The Storytelling Animal: How Stories Make Us Human.* Later prt. edition. Houghton Mifflin Harcourt, 2012.

Heath, Chip. *Made to Stick, Why Some Ideas Survive and Others Die.* Random House, 2007.

Karia, Akash. *TED Talks Storytelling: 23 Storytelling Techniques from the Best TED Talks, 3rd Edition.* CreateSpace Independent Publishing Platform, 2015.

Meyer Foundation, *Stories Worth Telling: A Guide to Strategic and Sustainable Nonprofit Storytelling* (Whitepaper).

Nossel, Murray, *Powered by Storytelling: Excavate, Craft, and Present Stories to Transform Business Communication,* 1 edition, McGraw-Hill Education, 2018.

Portnoy, Dan. *The Non-Profit Narrative: How Telling Stories Can Change the World*. PMG Press, 2012.

Zak, Paul, *The Moral Molecule: How Trust Works*, Reprint edition. Plume, 2013.

Articles

Bernstein, Elizabeth, *Wall Street Journal*, Why Good Storytellers are Happier in Life and Love, 7-4-2016

Websites and Blogs

Charitablegiftplanners.org

GLFHC.org, Greater Lawrence Family Health Center, *Storytelling the Mission*

Pentera.com

Rockefellerfoundation.org, *Telling and Spreading Stories That Fuel Change*

Southwest.com

TheGoodmanCenter.com

Printed in Great Britain
by Amazon